FAST TALK

Spanish

lonely planet

Fast Talk Spanish
1st edition – May 2004

Published by
Lonely Planet Publications Pty Ltd ABN 36 005 607 983
90 Maribyrnong St, Footscray, Victoria 3011, Australia

Lonely Planet Offices
Australia Locked Bag 1, Footscray, Victoria 3011
USA 150 Linden St, Oakland CA 94607
UK 72-82 Rosebery Ave, London, EC1R 4RW

Publisher Roz Hopkins
Publishing Manager Peter D'Onghia
Commissioning Editors Karin Vidstrup Monk, Karina Coates
Project Manager Fabrice Rocher
Series Designer Yukiyoshi Kamimura
Layout Designer Patrick Marris
Editors Francesca Coles, Meg Worby
Also thanks to Marta López

Photography
Flamenco dresses for sale in Granada, Andalucia (the home of flamenco).
by Christopher Wood. © Lonely Planet Images 2004

ISBN 1 74059 994 2

10 9 8 7 6 5 4 2 1

Printed by the Bookmaker International Ltd
Printed in China

CHAT 6

EXPLORE 13

SHOP 20

ENJOY 25

EAT & DRINK 27

CONTENTS

SERVICES 44

GO 48

SLEEP 56

WORK 60

HELP 62

LOOK UP 67

Language name: Spanish

Spanish is known to its native speakers as both *español*, **es·pa·*nyol***, and *castellano*, **kas·te·*lya*·no**.

Language family: Romance

Spanish belongs to the Romance family of languages and is a close relative of both Italian and Portuguese.

Key country & secondary countries:

Spanish is spoken not only in Spain but in many other countries all over the world. It's the language of most of Latin America and the West Indies as well as parts of Africa, the Phillipines, Guam and the US, making it one of the world's most widely spoken languages.

Approximate number of speakers:

There are some 390 million speakers of Spanish worldwide.

Donations to English:

English has borrowed numerous words from Spanish, including alligator, bonanza, canyon, guerilla and chocolate. Many of these borrowings are in turn derived from the indigenous languages of Latin America.

Grammar:

The structure of Spanish holds no major surprises for English speakers because the two languages are closely related.

Pronunciation:

Many Spanish sounds are similar to those found in English, so English speakers won't find making themselves understood in Spanish difficult.

Abbreviations used in this book:

m	masculine	sg	singular	pol	polite
f	feminine	pl	plural	inf	informal

CHAT

Meeting & greeting

Hello/Hi.	*Hola.*	*o*·la
Good morning.	*Buenos días.*	*bwe*·nos *dee*·as
Good afternoon. (until 8pm)	*Buenas tardes.*	*bwe*·nas *tar*·des
Good evening.	*Buenas noches.*	*bwe*·nas *no*·ches
See you later.	*Hasta luego.*	*as*·ta *lwe*·go
Goodbye/Bye.	*Adiós.*	a·*dyos*
How are you?	*¿Cómo está(s)?* pol/inf	*ko*·mo es·*ta(s)*
Fine, thanks.	*Bien, gracias.*	byen *gra*·thyas
Mr	*Señor*	se·*nyor*
Sir	*Don*	don
Ms/Mrs	*Señora*	se·*nyo*·ra
Madam	*Doña*	*do*·nya
Miss	*Señorita*	se·nyo·*ree*·ta

Essentials

Yes.	*Sí.*	see
No.	*No.*	no
Please.	*Por favor.*	por fa·*vor*
Thank you (very much).	*(Muchas) Gracias.*	(*moo*·chas) *gra*·thyas
You're welcome.	*De nada.*	de *na*·da
Excuse me.	*Perdón/Discúlpeme.*	per·*don*/dees·*kool*·pe·me
Sorry.	*Lo siento.*	lo *syen*·to

What's your name?

¿Cómo se llama Usted? pol — *ko*·mo se *lya*·ma oos·*te*

¿Cómo te llamas? inf — *ko*·mo te *lya*·mas

My name is ...

Me llamo ... — me *lya*·mo ...

I'd like to introduce you to ...

Quisiera presentarle a ... pol — kee·*sye*·ra pre·sen·*tar*·le a ...

Quisiera presentarte a ... inf — kee·*sye*·ra pre·sen·*tar*·te a ...

I'm pleased to meet you.

Mucho gusto. — *moo*·cho *goos*·to

It's been great meeting you.

Me ha encantado conocerle. pol — me a en·kan·*ta*·do ko·no·*ther*·le

Me ha encantado conocerte. inf — me a en·kan·*ta*·do ko·no·*ther*·te

This is my ...	*Éste/a es mi ...* m/f	*es*·te/a es mee ...
child	*hijo/a* m/f	*ee*·kho/a
colleague	*colega* m&f	ko·*le*·ga
friend	*amigo/a* m/f	a·*mee*·go/a
husband	*marido* m	ma·*ree*·do
partner (intimate)	*pareja* m&f	pa·*re*·kha
wife	*esposa* f	es·*po*·sa

I'm here ...	*Estoy aquí ...*	es·*toy* a·*kee* ...
for a holiday	*de vacaciones*	de va·ka·*thyo*·nes
on business	*en viaje de negocios*	en *vya*·khe de ne·*go*·thyos
to study	*estudiando*	es·too·*dyan*·do
with my family	*con mi familia*	kon mee fa·*mee*·lya
with my partner (intimate)	*con mi pareja*	kon mee pa·*re*·kha

How long are you here for?

¿Cuánto tiempo le va a quedar? pol — *kwan*·to *tyem*·po le va a ke·*dar*

¿Cuánto tiempo te vas a quedar? inf — *kwan*·to *tyem*·po te vas a ke·*dar*

I'm here for … days/weeks.		
	Estoy aquí por … días/ semanas.	es·*toy* a·*kee* por … *dee*·as/ se·*ma*·nas

For numbers, see the box feature in **LOOK UP**, page 67.

Here's my …	*Ésta es mi …*	*es*·ta es mee …
What's your …?	*¿Cuál es su/tu …?* pol/inf	kwal es soo/too …
address	*dirección*	dee·rek·*thyon*
email address	*dirección de email*	dee·rek·*thyon* de *ee*·mayl
fax number	*número de fax*	*noo*·me·ro de faks
home number	*número de teléfono*	*noo*·me·ro de te·*le*·fo·no
mobile number	*número de móvil*	*noo*·me·ro de *mo*·veel
work number	*número de teléfono en el trabajo*	*noo*·me·ro de te·*le*·fo·no en el tra·*ba*·kho

Breaking the language barrier

I speak a little Spanish.		
	Hablo un poco de español.	*ab*·lo oon *po*·ko de es·pa·*nyol*
Do you speak English?		
	¿Habla inglés?	*ab*·la een·*gles*
Does anyone speak English?		
	¿Hay alguien que hable inglés?	ai al·*gyen* ke *ab*·le een·*gles*
Do you understand?		
	¿Me entiende?	me en·*tyen*·de
I (don't) understand.		
	(No) Entiendo.	(no) en·*tyen*·do

How do you pronounce this word?
¿Cómo se pronuncia esta palabra? — ***ko***·mo se pro·***noon***·thya ***es***·ta pa·***lab***·ra

How do you write *'ciudad'*?
¿Cómo se escribe 'ciudad'? — ***ko***·mo se es·***kree***·be theew·***da***

What does ... mean?
¿Qué significa ...? — ke seeg·nee·***fee***·ka ...

Could you repeat that?
¿Puede repetir? — ***pwe***·de re·pe·***teer***

Could you please ...?	*¿Puede ..., por favor?*	***pwe***·de ... por fa·***vor***
speak more slowly	*hablar más despacio*	ab·***lar*** mas des·***pa***·thyo
write it down	*escribirlo*	es·kree·***beer***·lo

Personal details

Where are you from?
¿De dónde es/eres? pol/inf — de ***don***·de es/***e***·res

I'm from ...	*Soy de ...*	soy de ...
Australia	*Australia*	ow·***stra***·lya
Canada	*Canadá*	ka·na·***da***
England	*Inglaterra*	een·gla·***te***·ra
the USA	*los Estados Unidos*	los es·***ta***·dos oo·***nee***·dos

I'm ...	*Estoy ...*	es·***toy*** ...
married	*casado/a* m/f	ka·***sa***·do/a
separated	*separado/a* m/f	se·pa·***ra***·do/a
divorced	*divorciado/a* m/f	dee·vor·***thya***·do/a

I'm single.
Soy soltero/a. m/f — soy sol·***te***·ro/a

CHAT

Occupations & study

What do you do?

¿A qué le dedica? pol	a ke le de·*dee*·ka
¿A qué te dedicas? inf	a ke te de·*dee*·kas

I'm a/an …	*Soy …*	soy …
architect	*arquitecto/a* m/f	ar·kee·*tek*·to/a
teacher	*profesor/ profesora* m/f	pro·fe·*sor*/ pro·fe·*so*·ra
mechanic	*mecánico/a* m/f	me·*ka*·nee·ko/a
writer	*escritor/ escritora* m/f	es·kree·*tor*/ es·kree·*to*·ra

I work in …	*Trabajo en …*	tra·*ba*·kho en …
education	*enseñanza*	en·se·*nyan*·tha
hospitality	*hostelería*	os·te·le·*ree*·a
sales & marketing	*ventas y marketing*	*ven*·tas ee *mar*·ke·teen

I'm …	*Estoy …*	es·*toy* …
retired	*jubilado/a* m/f	khoo·bee·*la*·do/a
unemployed	*en el paro*	en el *pa*·ro

I'm studying …	*Estudio …*	es·*too*·dyo …
business	*comercio*	ko·*mer*·thyo
languages	*idiomas*	ee·*dyo*·mas
science	*ciencias*	*thyen*·thyas

What are you studying?

¿Qué estudia? pol	ke es·*too*·dya
¿Qué estudias? inf	ke es·*too*·dyas

For other occupations, see the dictionary in **LOOK UP**, page 70.

Age

How old ...?	*¿Cuántos años ...?*	*kwan*·tos *a*·nyos ...
are you	*tiene/tienes* pol/inf	*tye*·ne/*tye*·nes
is your daughter	*tiene su/tu hija* pol/inf	*tye*·ne soo/too *ee*·kha
is your son	*tiene su/tu hijo* pol/inf	*tye*·ne soo/too *ee*·kho

I'm ... years old.
Tengo ... años. — *ten*·go ... *a*·nyos

He/She is ... years old.
Él/Ella tiene ... años. — el/*e*·lya *tye*·ne ... *a*·nyos

For your age, see the numbers box in **LOOK UP**, page 67.

Feelings

I'm ...	*Tengo ...*	*ten*·go ...
I'm not ...	*No tengo ...*	no *ten*·go ...
Are you ...?	*¿Tiene/Tienes ...?* pol/inf	*tye*·ne/*tye*·nes ...
cold	*frio*	*free*·o
hot	*calor*	ka·*lor*
hungry	*hambre*	*am*·bre
in a hurry	*prisa*	*pree*·sa
thirsty	*sed*	se

I'm ...	*Estoy ...*	es·*toy* ...
I'm not ...	*No estoy ...*	no es·*toy* ...
Are you ...?	*¿Está/Estás ...?* pol/inf	es·*ta*/es·*tas* ...
annoyed	*fastidiado/a* m/f	fas·tee·*dya*·do/a
embarrassed	*avergonzado/a* m/f	a·ver·gon·*tha*·do/a
tired	*cansado/a* m/f	kan·*sa*·do/a
well	*bien*	byen

Beliefs

I'm (not) …	*(No) Soy …*	(no) soy …
agnostic	*agnóstico/a* m/f	ag·*nos*·tee·ko/a
Buddhist	*budista*	boo·*dees*·ta
Catholic	*católico/a* m/f	ka·*to*·lee·ko/a
Christian	*cristiano/a* m/f	krees·*tya*·no/a
Hindu	*hindú*	een·*doo*
Jewish	*judío/a* m/f	khoo·*dee*·o/a
Muslim	*musulmán/ musulmána* m/f	moo·sool·*man*/ moo·sool·*ma*·na
practising	*practicante*	prak·tee·*kan*·te
religious	*religioso/a* m/f	re·lee·*khyo*·so/a

Weather

What's the weather like?
¿Qué tiempo hace? — ke *tyem*·po *a*·the

(Today) It's raining.
(Hoy) Está lloviendo. — (oy) es·*ta* lyo·*vyen*·do

(Today) It's snowing.
(Hoy) Nieva. — (oy) *nye*·va

Today it's …	*Hoy hace …*	oy *a*·the …
Will it be … tomorrow?	*¿Mañana hará …?*	ma·*nya*·na a·*ra* …
cold	*frío*	*free*·o
freezing	*un frío que pela*	oon *free*·o ke *pe*·la
hot	*calor*	ka·*lor*
sunny	*sol*	sol
warm	*calor*	ka·*lor*
windy	*viento*	*vyen*·to

EXPLORE

Doing the sights

Do you have information on local places of interest?
¿Tiene información sobre los lugares de interés local? — **tye**·ne een·for·ma·**thyon** **so**·bre los loo·**ga**·res de een·te·**res** lo·**kal**

I have (one day).
Tengo (un día). — **ten**·go (oon **dee**·a)

Can we hire a guide?
¿Podemos alquilar un guía? — po·**de**·mos al·kee·**lar** oon **gee**·a

I'd like to see ...
Me gustaría ver ... — me goos·ta·**ree**·a ver ...

What's that?
¿Qué es eso? — ke es **e**·so

Who made it?
¿Quién lo hizo? — kyen lo **ee**·tho

How old is it?
¿De qué época es? — de ke **e**·po·ka es

I'd like a/an ...	*Quisiera ...*	kee·**sye**·ra ...
audio set	*un equipo audio*	oon e·**kee**·po **ow**·dyo
catalogue	*un catálogo*	oon ka·**ta**·lo·go
guidebook in English	*una guía turística en inglés*	**oo**·na **gee**·a too·**rees**·tee·ka en een·**gles**
(local) map	*un mapa (de la zona)*	oon **ma**·pa (de la **tho**·na)

Could you take a photograph of me?
¿Me puede/puedes hacer una foto? pol/inf — me **pwe**·de/**pwe**·des a·**ther** **oo**·na **fo**·to

EXPLORE

Can I take photographs (of you)?
¿(Le/Te) Puedo tomar fotos? pol/inf — (le/te) *pwe*·do to·*mar fo*·tos

I'll send you the photograph.
Le/Te mandaré la foto. pol/inf — le/te man·da·*re* la *fo*·to

Gallery & museum hopping

When's the … open?	*¿A qué hora abre …?*	a ke *o*·ra *a*·bre …
gallery	*la galería*	la ga·le·*ree*·a
museum	*el museo*	el moo·*se*·o

What's in the collection?
¿Qué hay en la colección? — ke ai en la ko·lek·*thyon*

What kind of art are you interested in?
¿Qué tipo de arte le/te interesa? pol/inf — ke *tee*·po de *ar*·te le/te een·te·*re*·sa

I'm interested in …
Me interesa/interesan … sg/pl — me een·te·*re*·sa/een·te·*re*·san …

What do you think of …?
¿Qué piensa/piensas de …? pol/inf — ke *pyen*·sa/*pyen*·sas de …

It's a/an exhibition of …
Es una exposición de … — es *oo*·na eks·po·see·*thyon* de …

I like the works of …
Me gustan las obras de … — me *goos*·tan las *o*·bras de …

It reminds me of …
Me recuerda a … — me re·*kwer*·da a …

… art	*arte …*	*ar*·te …
graphic	*gráfico*	*gra*·fee·ko
impressionist	*impresionista*	eem·pre·syo·*nees*·ta
modernist	*modernista*	mo·der·*nees*·ta
Renaissance	*renacentista*	re·na·then·*tees*·ta

EXPLORE

Getting in

What time does it open?
¿A qué hora abren? — a ke *o*·ra *ab*·ren

What time does it close?
¿A qué hora cierran? — a ke *o*·ra *thye*·ran

What's the admission charge?
¿Cuánto cuesta la entrada? — *kwan*·to *kwes*·ta la en·*tra*·da

It costs (seven euros).
Cuesta (siete euros). — *kwes*·ta (*sye*·te e·oo·ros)

Is there a discount for ...?	*¿Hay descuentos para ...?*	ai des·*kwen*·tos *pa*·ra ...
children	*niños*	*nee*·nyos
families	*familias*	fa·*mee*·lee·as
groups	*grupos*	*groo*·pos
pensioners	*pensionistas*	pen·syo·*nees*·tas
students	*estudiantes*	es·too·*dyan*·tes

Tours

Can you recommend a ...?	*¿Puede recomendar algún/algúna ...?* m/f	*pwe*·de re·ko·men·*dar* al·*goon*/al·*goo*·na ...
boat trip	*paseo* m *en barca*	pa·*se*·o en *bar*·ka
excursion	*excursión* f	eks·koor·*syon*
tour	*recorrido* m	re·ko·*ree*·do

When's the next ...?	*¿Cuándo es el/la próximo/a ...?* m/f	*kwan*·do es el/la *prok*·see·mo/a ...
boat trip	*paseo* m *en barca*	pa·*se*·o en *bar*·ka
excursion	*excursión* f	eks·koor·*syon*
tour	*recorrido* m	re·ko·*ree*·do

Do I need to take ... with me? *¿Necesito llevar ...?* ne·the·*see*·to lye·*var* ...

Is ... included? *¿Incluye ...?* een·*kloo*·ye ...

accommodation	*el alojamiento*	el a·lo·kha·*myen*·to
the admission charge	*el precio de entrada*	el *pre*·thyo de en·*tra*·da
equipment	*equipo*	e·*kee*·po
food	*comida*	ko·*mee*·da
transport	*transporte*	trans·*por*·te

Can we hire a guide?
¿Podemos alquilar un guía? po·*de*·mos al·kee·*lar* oon *gee*·a

The guide will pay.
El guía va a pagar. el *gee*·a va a pa·*gar*

The guide has paid.
El guía ha pagado. el *gee*·a a pa·*ga*·do

Do I need to take (lunch) with me?
¿Necesito llevar (el almuerzo)? ne·the·*see*·to lye·*var* (el al·*mwer*·tho)

How long is the tour?
¿Cuánto dura el recorrido? *kwan*·to *doo*·ra el re·ko·*ree*·do

What time should I be back?
¿A qué hora tengo que volver? a ke *o*·ra *ten*·go ke vol·*ver*

Be back here at ...
Vuelva a ... *vwel*·va ...

I'm with them.
Voy con ellos. voy kon *e*·lyos

I've lost my group.
He perdido mi grupo. e per·*dee*·do mee *groo*·po

Have you seen a group of (Australians).
¿Ha visto un grupo de (Australianos)? a *vees*·to oon *groo*·po de (ow·stra·*lya*·nos)

Top 6 day trips

Sometimes the frenzied pace of Barcelona and Madrid can get a little overwhelming. For a more relaxing alternative, head out of town to enjoy a quieter, off-the-beaten-track cultural experience.

Barcelona

Montserrat — mont·se·*rat*

This remarkable massif of limestone pinnacles rising over deep gorges is also the spiritual heart of Catalonia. Thousands of people visit the Monastery of Montserrat each year to venerate the statue of *La Moreneta* (the Black Virgin).

Sitges — *seet*·ges

This seaside resort town is a summertime mecca for fashionable city folk and a huge international gay set. In the 1890s it was a trendy bohemian hang-out and it has remained one of Spain's most unconventional resorts.

Teatre-Museu Dalí — te·*a*·tre moo·*se*·oo da·*lee*

Situated at Figueres, Dalí's birthplace, the museum comprises three floors of tricks, illusions and absurdities which allow the visitor to wander through one of the most fertile imaginations of the 20th century.

Madrid

Real Palacio de Aranjuez — re·*al* pa·*la*·thyo de a·*ran*·khweth

Once a royal playground, this vast and richly decorated palace and its meticulously maintained gardens make a popular weekend getaway.

San Lorenzo de El Escorial — san lo·*ren*·tho de el es·ko·*ryal*

Sheltering at the foot of the Sierra de Guadarrama this magnificent 16th century complex consisting of a huge monastery, royal palace and mausoleum is a must-see. Among the artistic riches on display are a crucifix by Benvenuto Cellini and paintings by El Greco, Titian, Tintoretto and Bosch.

Toledo — to·*le*·do

Situated on a hilltop in a bend of the River Tajo, Toledo is a remarkably beautiful city. It's a treasure trove of architectural history with its labyrinthine medieval streets, alcazar (Moorish fortified palace) and stunning cathedral.

Top 10 sights

It would take a lifetime to explore all the wonders of the vibrant arts and culture of both Barcelona and Madrid. If you don't have that much time on your hands, make sure you pack in a few of these famous highlights:

Barcelona

Fundación Joan Miró foon·da·*syon zho*·an mee·*ro*

The largest single collection of the painter Joan Miró's work is housed in a magnificent building designed by his friend Josep Luís Sert. The combination of natural light, white walls and airy galleries make this a wonderful setting to appreciate the works of Catalonia's greatest artist.

La Sagrada Família la sa·*gra*·da fa·*mee*·lya

Designed by Gaudí, this half-complete church with its soaring towers and detailed, textured facades is emblematic of Barcelona and is the most visited unfinished building site in the world. This colossal edifice takes up a whole block of the l'Eixample district and has its own metro station.

Manzana de la Discordia man·*sa*·na de la dees·*kor*·dya

This remarkable stretch of Passeig de Gràcia is called the 'Block of Discord', because you'll find wildly contrasting works of the three greatest architects of Modernisme on it. Domènech i Montaner, Puig i Cadafalch and Gaudí were hired by the city's most well-heeled families to have their houses remodelled in the hip new style.

Palau de la Música Catalana pa·*low* de la *moo*·see·ka ka·ta·*la*·na

This concert hall is one of Barcelona's most brilliant highlights and is celebrated by many as the crowning glory of Modernisme. The bare brick facade of mosaics, tile-clad pillars and busts only hints at the richness of the decoration of the interior. The auditorium is a splendid symphony of ceramics and stained glass.

Parc Güell park goo·*el*

The park where Gaudí turned his hand to landscape gardening is one of the most wonderful on the planet – a jovial and enchanting spot to relax. Gaudí's inimitable style has created a place where the artificial almost seems more natural than the endeavours of Mother Nature. The park contains a wonderful esplanade, the centrepiece of which is the Banc de Trencadis, a delightful bench that curves around its perimeter and is clad with ceramics.

Madrid

Campo del Moro *kam*·po del *mo*·ro

This exquisite park laid out in the English style was once a playground for royal children. Among the greenery you'll find winding paths, verdant canopies, neatly laid-out flower beds, fountains and wandering peacocks.

Museo del Prado moo·*the*·o del *pra*·do

The staggering richness of the Museo del Prado's collection is a reason in itself for many people to come to Madrid. Its three floors are packed with masterpieces with the works of Spanish masters El Greco, Goya and Velasquez featuring prominently.

Palacio Real pa·*la*·thyo re·*al*

This vast Italianate palace, commenced by Felipe V, comprises some 2800 rooms, 50 of which are open to the general public. The interiors are a marvel of sumptuous decoration.

Plaza de la Villa *pla*·tha de la *vee*·lya

Thought to have been the city's permanent seat of government in the Middle Ages, this square is one of Madrid's most beautiful spots, with a sense of history and some fine architecture including the 15th century Casa de los Lujanes.

Plaza Mayor *pla*·tha ma·*yor*

The imperial heart of Madrid beats loudest at this town square. Once the site of royal festivities, bullfights and *autos-da-fé* (the ritual condemnation and burning of herectics) it's now given over to those fancying an alfresco drink or snack, or wanting to rendezvous in an obvious location.

SHOP
Essentials

Where's . . .?	*¿Dónde está(n) . . .?* sg/pl	**don·de es·*ta(n)* . . .**
a bank	*un banco* sg	**oon *ban*·ko**
a department store	*unos grandes almacenes* pl	***oo*·nos *gran*·des al·ma·*the*·nes**
a supermarket	*un supermercado* sg	**oon soo·per·mer·*ka*·do**

Where can I buy . . .?
¿Dónde puedo comprar . . .? **don·de *pwe*·do kom·*prar* . . .**

I'd like to buy . . .
Quisiera comprar . . . **kee·*sye*·ra kom·*prar* . . .**

I'm just looking.
Sólo estoy mirando. ***so*·lo es·*toy* mee·*ran*·do**

Can I look at it?
¿Puedo verlo? ***pwe*·do *ver*·lo**

Do you have any others?
¿Tiene otros? ***tye*·ne *o*·tros**

Could I have a bag, please?
¿Podría darme una bolsa, por favor? **po·*dree*·a *dar*·me *oo*·na *bol*·sa por fa·*vor***

Could I have it wrapped?
¿Me lo podría envolver? **me lo po·*dree*·a en·vol·*ver***

Does it have a guarantee?
¿Tiene garantía? ***tye*·ne ga·ran·*tee*·a**

Can I have it sent overseas?
¿Pueden enviarlo por correo a otro país? ***pwe*·den en·vee·*ar*·lo por ko·*re*·o a *o*·tro pa·*ees***

SHOP

Can I pick it up later?
¿Puedo recogerlo más tarde? **pwe·do re·ko·*kher*·lo mas *tar*·de**

It's faulty.
Es defectuoso. **es de·fek·too·*o*·so**

I'd like …, please.	*Quisiera …, por favor.*	**kee·*sye*·ra … por fa·*vor***
my money back	*que me devuelva el dinero*	**ke me de·*vwel*·va el dee·*ne*·ro**
to return this	*devolver esto*	**de·vol·*ver es*·to**

Hot shop spots

Shopping in Spain is a retail revelation. Barcelona reportedly boasts the highest number of shops per person in Europe. Madrid, too, is a shopper's paradise with everything from tiny specialist stores to mammoth malls. In both cities it's the quality that impresses most.

Barri Gòtic, Barcelona – groovy street, club & second hand wear • antique shops • quirky speciality shops

El Raval, Barcelona – design & fashion outlets • alternative clothes & music

La Ribera, Barcelona – artisan workshops

l'Eixample, Barcelona – local & international boutiques • jewellery stores

Chueca, Madrid – an excellent shopping precinct with fashionable shops

Plaza Mayor, Madrid – gifts • items typical of Madrid

Salamanca, Madrid – similar to Chueca but with more expensive, conservative tastes catered for

Paying

How much is this?

¿Cuánto cuesta esto?	***kwan***·to ***kwes***·ta ***es***·to

Can you write down the price?

¿Puede escribir el precio?	***pwe***·de es·kree·***beer*** el ***pre***·thyo

That's too expensive.

Es muy caro.	es mooy ***ka***·ro

I'll give you ...

Le daré ...	le da·***re*** ...

Do you have something cheaper?

¿Tiene algo más barato?	***tye***·ne ***al***·go mas ba·***ra***·to

Can I have smaller notes?

¿Me lo puede dar en billetes más pequeños?	me lo ***pwe***·de dar en bee·***lye***·tes mas pe·***ke***·nyos

I'd like my change, please.

Quisiera mi cambio, por favor.	kee·***sye***·ra mee ***kam***·byo por fa·***vor***

Do you accept ...?	*¿Aceptan ...?*	a·***thep***·tan ...
credit cards	*tarjetas de crédito*	tar·***khe***·tas de ***kre***·dee·to
debit cards	*tarjetas de débito*	tar·***khe***·tas de ***de***·bee·to
travellers cheques	*cheques de viajero*	***che***·kes de vya·***khe***·ro

Could I have a ..., please?	*¿Podría darme ..., por favor?*	po·***dree***·a ***dar***·me ... por fa·***vor***
bag	*una bolsa*	***oo***·na ***bol***·sa
receipt	*un recibo*	oon re·***thee***·bo

Clothes & shoes

I'm looking for …	*Busco …*	*boos*·ko …
jeans	*vaqueros*	va·*ke*·ros
shoes	*zapatos*	tha·*pa*·tos
underwear	*ropa interior*	*ro*·pa een·te·*ryor*
small	*pequeña*	pe·*ke*·nya
medium	*mediana*	me·*dya*·na
large	*grande*	*gran*·de

Can I try it on?
¿Me lo puedo probar? — me lo *pwe*·do pro·*bar*

My size is (42).
Uso la talla (cuarenta y dos). — *oo*·so la *ta*·lya (kwa·*ren*·ta ee dos)

It doesn't fit.
No me queda bien. — no me *ke*·da byen

Books & music

Is there a/an (English-language) …?	*¿Hay algún/alguna … (en inglés)?* m/f	ai al·*goon*/al·*goo*·na … (en een·*gles*)
book by …	*libro* m *de …*	*lee*·bro de …
bookshop	*librería* m	lee·bre·*ree*·a
entertainment guide	*guía* f *del ocio*	*gee*·a del *o*·thyo
section	*sección* f	sek·*thyon*
I'd like (a) …	*Quisiera …*	kee·*sye*·ra …
blank tape	*una cinta virgen*	*oo*·na *theen*·ta *veer*·khen
CD	*un cómpact*	oon *kom*·pakt
headphones	*unos auriculares*	*oo*·nos ow·ree·koo·*la*·res

I'd like (a) ...	*Quisiera ...*	**kee·*sye*·ra ...**
map	*un mapa*	**oon *ma*·pa**
newspaper (in English)	*un periódico (en inglés)*	**oon pe·*ryo*·dee·ko (en een·*gles*)**
some paper	*papel*	**pa·*pel***
pen	*un bolígrafo*	**oon bo·*lee*·gra·fo**
postcard	*una postal*	***oo*·na pos·*tal***

I heard a band called ...
Escuché a un grupo que se llama ... — **es·koo·*che* a oon *groo*·po ke se *lya*·ma ...**

What's their best recording?
¿Cuál es su mejor disco? — **kwal es soo me·*khor dees*·ko**

Can I listen to this?
¿Puedo escuchar este aquí? — ***pwe*·do es·koo·*char es*·te a·*kee***

Photography

I need ... film for this camera.	*Necesito película ... para esta cámara.*	**ne·the·*see*·to pe·*lee*·koo·la ... *pa*·ra es·ta *ka*·ma·ra**
APS	*APS*	**a pe *e*·se**
B&W	*en blanco y negro*	**en *blan*·ko y *ne*·gro**
colour	*en color*	**en ko·*lor***
(400) speed	*de sensibilidad (cuatrocientos)*	**de sen·see·bee·lee·*da* (*kwa*·tro·*thyen*·tos)**

How much is it to develop this film?
¿Cuánto cuesta revelar este carrete? — ***kwan*·to *kwes*·ta re·ve·*lar es*·te ka·*re*·te**

When will it be ready?
¿Cuándo estará listo? — ***kwan*·do es·ta·*ra lees*·to**

ENJOY

What's on?

What's on . . .?	*¿Qué hay . . .?*	**ke ai . . .**
locally	*en la zona*	**en la *tho*·na**
this weekend	*este fin de semana*	***es*·te feen de se·*ma*·na**
today	*hoy*	**oy**
tonight	*esta noche*	***es*·ta *no*·che**
Where are . . .?	*¿Dónde hay . . .?*	***don*·de ai . . .**
gay venues	*lugares gay*	**loo·*ga*·res ge**
places to eat	*lugares para comer*	**loo·*ga*·res *pa*·ra ko·*mer***
pubs	*pubs*	**poobs**
Is there a local . . . guide?	*¿Hay una guía . . . de la zona?*	**ai *oo*·na *gee*·a . . . de la *tho*·na**
entertainment	*del ocio*	**del *o*·thyo**
film	*de cine*	**de *thee*·ne**
I feel lIke going to a . . .	*Tengo ganas de ir . . .*	***ten*·go *ga*·nas de eer . . .**
ballet	*al ballet*	**al ba·*le***
bar	*a un bar*	**a oon bar**
café	*a un café*	**a oon ka·*fe***
concert	*a un concierto*	**a oon kon·*thyer*·to**
karaoke bar	*a un bar de karaoke*	**a oon bar de ka·ra·*o*·ke**
nightclub	*a una discoteca*	**a *oo*·na dees·ko·*te*·ka**
party	*a una fiesta*	**a *oo*·na *fyes*·ta**
restaurant	*a un restaurante*	**a oon res·tow·*ran*·te**

Meeting up

What time shall we meet?		
¿A qué hora quedamos?		**a ke *o*·ra ke·*da*·mos**
Where will we meet?		
¿Dónde quedamos?		***don*·de ke·*da*·mos**

Let's meet …	*Quedamos …*	**ke·*da*·mos …**
at (eight) o'clock	*a (las ocho)*	**a (las *o*·cho)**
at the (entrance)	*en (la entrada)*	**en (la en·*tra*·da)**

Small talk

I (don't) like …	*(No) Me gusta …*	**(no) me *goos*·ta …**
dancing	*ir a bailar*	**eer a bai·*lar***
films	*el cine*	**el *thee*·ne**
music	*la música*	**la *moo*·see·ka**
pub crawls	*ir de bar en bar*	**eer de bar en bar**
shopping	*ir de compras*	**eer de *kom*·pras**

Do you like to …?	*¿Le/Te gusta …?* pol/inf	**le/te *goos*·ta …**
go to concerts	*ir a conciertos*	**eer a kon·*thyer*·tos**
listen to music	*escuchar música*	**es·koo·*char* *moo*·see·ka**
sing	*cantar*	***kan*·tar**

I (don't) like …	*(No) Me gusta/ gustan …* sg/pl	**(no) me *goos*·ta/ *goos*·tan …**
animated films	*películas* pl *de dibujos animados*	**pe·*lee*·koo·las de dee·*boo*·khos a·nee·*ma*·dos**
horror movies	*cine* sg *de terror*	***thee*·ne de te·*ror***
sci-fi films	*cine* sg *de ciencia ficción*	***thee*·ne de *thyen*·thya feek·*thyon***

EAT & DRINK

breakfast	*desayuno* m	de·sa·*yoo*·no
lunch	*almuerzo* m	al·*mwer*·tho
dinner	*cena* f	*the*·na
snack	*tentempié* m	ten·tem·*pye*
eat	*comer*	ko·*mer*
drink	*beber*	be·*ber*

Choosing & booking

Can you recommend a ...?	*¿Puede recomendar un ...?*	*pwe*·de re·ko·men·*dar* oon ...
bar	*bar*	bar
café	*café*	ka·*fe*
restaurant	*restaurante*	res·tow·*ran*·te
Where would you go for ...?	*¿Adónde se va para ...?*	a·*don*·de se va *pa*·ra ...
a celebration	*celebrar*	the·le·*brar*
a cheap meal	*comer barato*	ko·*mer* ba·*ra*·to
local specialities	*comer comida típica*	ko·*mer* ko·*mee*·da *tee*·pee·ka
I'd like ..., please.	*Quisiera ..., por favor.*	kee·*sye*·ra ... por fa·*vor*
the (non)smoking section	*(no) fumadores*	(no) foo·ma·*do*·res
a table for (five)	*una mesa para (cinco)*	*oo*·na *me*·sa *pa*·ra (*theen*·ko)

Eateries

Restaurants have been part of Spanish culture for centuries and you'll find a diverse selection of fantastic places to eat. Sample the local flavours at some of these eateries:

horno asador **_or_·no a·sa·_dor_**
the quintessential Spanish restaurant centered around a massive wood-fired meat-roasting oven that imparts an atmospheric glow and an aroma to set carnivorous taste buds on fire

terraza **te·_ra_·tha**
an al fresco restaurant, often with a small interior dining room, usually found clustered together with other *terrazas* (offering very similar menus) in city centres

restaurante **res·tow·_ran_·te**
a proper sit-down restaurant much like any other in the Western world except that in Spain they tend to be small and intimate and more of a social institution

casa de comidas **_ka_·sa de ko·_mee_·das**
a working-class restaurant that serves cheap, wholesome meals with excellent service

tasca **_tas_·ka**
a tapas bar, sometimes the bar of a proper restaurant, where you can expect to find a lively atmosphere and a counter groaning with aromatic, mouth-watering self-serve tapas

jamónería **kha·mon·e·_ree_·a**
a shrine to the Spanish passion for ham, the interior of this, ironically, seafood restaurant is festooned with countless legs of sweet-smelling ham which are consumed as appetisers

Ordering

What would you recommend?		
¿Qué recomienda?		**ke re·ko·*myen*·da**

Please bring …	*Por favor nos trae …*	**por fa·*vor* nos *tra*·e …**
the bill	*la cuenta*	**la *kwen*·ta**
the drink list	*la lista de bebidas*	**la *lees*·ta de be·*bee*·das**
the menu	*el menú*	**el me·*noo***

I'd like it …	*Lo quiero …*	**lo *kye*·ro …**
medium	*no muy hecho*	**no mooy *e*·cho**
rare	*vuelta y vuelta*	***vwel*·ta ee *vwel*·ta**
steamed	*al vapor*	**al va·*por***
well-done	*muy hecho*	**mooy *e*·cho**
with the dressing on the side	*con el aliño aparte*	**kon el a·*lee*·nyo a·*par*·te**
with/without …	*con/sin …*	**kon/seen …**

Nonalcoholic drinks

(cup of) coffee …	*(taza de) café* **m** *…*	**(*ta*·tha de) ka·*fe* …**
(cup of) tea …	*(taza de) té* **m** *…*	**(*ta*·tha de) te …**
with milk	*con leche*	**kon *le*·che**
with/without sugar	*con/sin azúcar*	**kon/seen a·*thoo*·kar**

(orange) juice	*zumo* **m** *de (naranja)*	***zoo*·mo de (na·*ran*·kha)**
soft drink	*refresco* **m**	**re·*fres*·ko**

… water	*agua* **f** *…*	***a*·gwa …**
boiled	*hervida*	**er·*vee*·da**
(sparkling) mineral	*mineral (con gas)*	**mee·ne·*ral* (kon gas)**

Alcoholic drinks

beer	*cerveza* f	ther·*ve*·tha
brandy	*coñac* m	ko·*nyak*
champagne	*champán* m	cham·*pan*
cocktail	*combinado* m	kom·bee·*na*·do
sangria (red-wine punch)	*sangría* f	san·*gree*·a
bottle/glass of ... wine	*botella/copa* f *de vino ...*	bo·*te*·lya/*ko*·pa de *vee*·no ...
dessert	*dulce*	*dool*·the
red	*tinto*	*teen*·to
rosé	*rosado*	ro·*sa*·do
sparkling	*espumoso*	es·poo·*mo*·so
white	*blanco*	*blan*·ko
... of beer	*... de cerveza*	... de ther·*ve*·tha
glass	*caña* f	*ka*·nya
jug	*jarra* f	*kha*·ra
pint	*pinta* f	*peen*·ta
shot of (whisky)	*chupito* m *de (güisqui)*	choo·*pee*·to de (*gwees*·kee)

In the bar

I'll have ...
Para mí ... — *pa*·ra mee ...

Same again, please.
Otra de lo mismo. — *o*·tra de lo *mees*·mo

I'll buy you a drink.
Le/Te invito a una copa. pol/inf — le/te een·*vee*·to a *oo*·na *ko*·pa

What would you like?
¿Qué quiere(s) tomar? pol/inf — ke *kye*·re(s) to·*mar*

It's my round.
Es mi ronda. — es mee *ron*·da

How much is that?
¿Cuánto es eso? — *kwan*·to es *e*·so

Cheers!
¡Salud! — sa·*loo*

Buying food

How much is (a kilo of cheese)?
¿Cuánto vale (un kilo de queso)? — *kwan*·to *va*·le (oon *kee*·lo de *ke*·so)

What's the local speciality?
¿Cuál es la especialidad de la zona? — kwal es la es·pe·thya·lee·*da* de la *tho*·na

What's that?
¿Qué es eso? — ke es *e*·so

I'd like ...	*Póngame ...*	*pon*·ga·me ...
(200) grams	*(doscientos) gramos*	(dos·*thyen*·tos) *gra*·mos
(two) kilos	*(dos) kilos*	(dos) *kee*·los
(three) pieces	*(tres) piezas*	(tres) *pye*·thas
(six) slices	*(seis) lonchas*	(seys) *lon*·chas
that one	*ése/a* m/f	*e*·se/a
two	*dos*	dos

Less, please.	*Menos, por favor.*	*me*·nos por fa·*vor*
Enough, thanks.	*Basta, gracias.*	*ba*·sta *gra*·thyas
More, please.	*Más, por favor.*	mas por fa·*vor*

Special diets & allergies

Is there a (vegetarian) restaurant near here?

¿Hay un restaurante (vegetariano) por aquí?	ai oon res·tow·*ran*·te (ve·khe·ta·*rya*·no) por a·*kee*

I'm vegetarian.

Soy vegetariano/a. m/f	soy ve·khe·ta·*rya*·no/a

I'm vegan.

Soy vegetariano/a estricto/a. m/f	soy ve·khe·ta·*rya*·no/a es·*treek*·to/a

I don't eat (red meat).

No como (carne roja).	no *ko*·mo (*kar*·ne *ro*·kha)

Could you prepare a meal without ...?	*¿Me puede preparar una comida sin ...?*	me *pwe*·de pre·pa·*rar* *oo*·na ko·*mee*·da seen ...
butter	*mantequilla*	man·te·*kee*·lya
eggs	*huevo*	*we*·vo
fish	*pescado*	pes·*ka*·do
meat/ fish stock	*caldo de carne/ pescado*	*kal*·do de *kar*·ne/ pes·*ka*·do
pork	*cerdo*	*ther*·do
poultry	*aves*	*a*·ves

I'm allergic to ...	*Soy alérgico/a ...* m/f	soy a·*ler*·khee·ko/a ...
dairy produce	*a los productos lácteos*	a los pro·*dook*·tos *lak*·te·os
eggs	*a los huevos*	a los *we*·vos
MSG	*al glutamato monosódico*	al gloo·ta·*ma*·to mo·no·*so*·dee·ko
nuts	*a las nueces*	a las *nwe*·thes
seafood	*a los mariscos*	a los ma·*rees*·kos
shellfish	*a los crustáceos*	a los kroos·*ta*·thyos

On the menu

Aperitivos	a·pe·ree·*tee*·vos	appetisers
Caldos	*kal*·dos	soups
De Entrada	de en·*tra*·da	entrées
Ensaladas	en·sa·*la*·das	salads
Segundos Platos	se·*goon*·dos *pla*·tos	main courses
Postres	*pos*·tres	desserts
Cervezas	ther·*ve*·thas	beers
Licores	lee·*ko*·res	spirits
Refrescos	re·*fres*·kos	soft drinks
Vinos Blancos	*vee*·nos *blan*·kos	white wines
Vinos Dulces	*vee*·nos *dool*·thes	dessert wines
Vinos Espumosos	*vee*·nos es·poo·*mo*·sos	sparkling wines
Vinos Tintos	*vee*·nos *teen*·tos	red wines
Digestivos	dee·khes·*tee*·vos	digestifs

For more help reading the menu, see the **Menu decoder** below.

Menu decoder

a la plancha	a la *plan*·cha	grilled • on a griddle
a la vasca	a la *vas*·ka	in a Basque green sauce
aceite m	a·*they*·te	oil
aceitunas f pl	a·they·*too*·nas	olives
— *rellenas*	re·*lye*·nas	stuffed olives
acelgas f pl	a·*thel*·gas	chard (a variety of beet)
adobo	a·*do*·bo	battered
aguacate m	a·gwa·*ka*·te	avocado
ahumado/a m/f	a·oo·*ma*·do/a	smoked
ajo m	*a*·kho	garlic
al ajillo	al a·*khee*·lyo	in garlic
al horno	al *or*·no	baked

albaricoque m	al·ba·ree·*ko*·ke	apricot
albóndigas f pl	al·*bon*·dee·gas	meatballs
alcachofa f	al·ka·*cho*·fa	artichoke
allioli m	a·*lyo*·lee	garlic sauce
almejas f pl	al·*me*·khas	clams
almendra f	al·*men*·dra	almond
alubias f pl	a·*loo*·byas	kidney beans
anchoas f pl	an·*cho*·as	anchovies
anguila f	an·*gwee*·la	eel
anís m	a·*nees*	anise
apio m	*a*·pyo	celery
arroz m	a·*roth*	rice
— con leche	kon *le*·che	rice pudding
asado/a m/f	a·*sa*·do/a	roasted
atún m	a·*toon*	tuna
bacalao m	ba·ka·*low*	salted cod
beicon m *con queso*	*bey*·kon kon *ke*·so	cold bacon with cheese
berberechos m pl	ber·be·*re*·chos	cockles
berenjena f	be·ren·*khe*·na	aubergine • eggplant
besugo m	be·*soo*·go	bream
bistec m	bee·*stek*	steak
— con patatas	kon pa·*ta*·tas	steak & chips
blanco m	*blan*·ko	white
bocadillo m	bo·ka·*dee*·lyo	tapas in a sandwich
bollos m pl	*bo*·lyos	bread rolls
boquerones m pl	bo·ke·*ro*·nes	anchovies
— en vinagre	en vee·*na*·gre	anchovies in vinaigrette
boquerones m pl *fritos*	bo·ke·*ro*·nes *free*·tos	fried anchovies
brasa	*bra*·sa	chargrilled
buey m	bwey	ox
butifarra f	boo·tee·*fa*·ra	thick sausage
cabra f	*ka*·bra	goat
cacahuete m	ka·ka·*we*·te	peanut

café m	ka·*fe*	coffee
— ***con leche***	kon *le*·che	coffee with milk
— ***cortado***	kor·*ta*·do	coffee with a little milk
— ***descafeinado***	des·ka·fey·*na*·do	decaffeinated coffee
— ***helado***	e·*la*·do	iced coffee
— ***solo***	so·lo	black coffee
calabacín m	ka·la·ba·*theen*	courgette • zucchini
calabaza f	ka·la·*ba*·tha	pumpkin
calamares m pl	ka·la·*ma*·res	calamari • squid
— ***a la romana***	a la ro·*ma*·na	calamari • squid rings fried in butter
caldereta f	kal·de·*re*·ta	stew
caldo m	*kal*·do	broth • consommé • stock
callos m pl	*ka*·lyos	tripe
camarón m	ka·ma·*ron*	shrimp • small prawn
canelones m pl	ka·ne·*lo*·nes	cannelloni
cangrejo m	kan·*gre*·kho	crab
— ***de río***	de *ree*·o	crayfish
carabinero m	ka·ra·bee·*ne*·ro	large prawn
caracol m	ka·ra·*kol*	snail
carajillo m	ka·ra·*khee*·lyo	coffee with liqueur
carne f	*kar*·ne	meat
caza f	*ka*·tha	game (meat)
cazuela f	ka·*thwe*·la	casserole
cebolla f	the·*bo*·lya	onion
cerdo m	*ther*·do	pork
cereales m pl	the·re·*a*·les	cereal
cereza f	the·*re*·tha	cherry
champiñones m pl	cham·pee·*nyo*·nes	mushrooms
— ***al ajillo***	al a·*khee*·lyo	garlic mushrooms
chanquetes m pl	chan·*ke*·tes	whitebait
charcutería f	char·koo·te·*ree*·a	cured pork meats • shop selling them
chipirón m	chee·pee·*ron*	small squid
chivo m	*chee*·vo	kid

choco m	*cho*·ko	cuttlefish
chorizo m	cho·*ree*·tho	spicy red or white sausage
— al horno	al *or*·no	baked spicy *chorizo*
chuleta f	choo·*le*·ta	chop • cutlet
churrasco m	choo·*ras*·ko	grilled meat or ribs in a tangy sauce • Galician meat dish
churro m	*choo*·ro	long, deep-fried doughnut
churros m pl *con chocolate*	*choo*·ros kon cho·ko·*la*·te	fried pastry strips for dunking in hot chocolate
ciruela f	theer·*we*·la	plum
cochinillo m	ko·chee·*nee*·lyo	suckling pig
cocido m	ko·*thee*·do	cooked • stew made with chickpeas, pork & chorizo
cocina f	ko·*thee*·na	kitchen
coco m	*ko*·ko	coconut
col m	kol	cabbage
coles m pl *de bruselas*	*ko*·les de broo·*se*·las	Brussels sprouts
coliflor f	ko·lee·*flor*	cauliflower
conejo m	ko·*ne*·kho	rabbit
cordero m	kor·*de*·ro	lamb
costillas f pl	kos·*tee*·lyas	ribs
croquetas f pl	kro·*ke*·tas	fried croquettes, often filled with ham or chicken
crudo/a m/f	kroo·do/a	raw
cuajada f	kwa·*kha*·da	milk junket with honey
doble m	*do*·ble	long black coffee
dorada f	do·*ra*·da	sea bass
dulce	*dool*·the	sweet
empanada f	em·pa·*na*·da	pie
ensaimada f	en·sai·*ma*·da	sweet bread (made of lard)
ensalada f	en·sa·*la*·da	salad
ensaladilla f	en·sa·la·*dee*·lya	vegetable salad
— rusa	*roo*·sa	vegetable salad with mayonnaise

entremeses m	en·tre·*me*·ses	hors d'oeuvres
escabeche m	es·ka·*be*·che	pickled or marinated fish
espárragos m pl	es·*pa*·ra·gos	asparagus
espagueti m	es·pa·*ge*·tee	spaghetti
espinacas f pl	es·pee·*na*·kas	spinach
estofado m	es·to·*fa*·do	stew
estofado/a m/f	es·to·*fa*·do/a	braised
faba f	*fa*·ba	type of dried bean
faisán m	fai·*san*	pheasant
fideos m pl	fee·*de*·os	thin pasta noodles with sauce
filete m	fee·*le*·te	fillet
filete m *empanado*	fee·*le*·te em·pa·*na*·do	pork, cheese & ham wrapped in breadcrumbs & fried
flan m	flan	crème caramel
frambuesa f	fram·*bwe*·sa	raspberry
fresa f	*fre*·sa	strawberry
fresco/a m/f	*fres*·ko/a	fresh
frijol m	*free*·khol	dried bean
frito/a m/f	*free*·to/a	fried
fruta f	*froo*·ta	fruit
fuerte	*fwer*·te	strong
gachos m pl	*ga*·chos	type of porridge
galleta f	ga·*lye*·ta	biscuit • cookie
gambas f pl	*gam*·bas	prawns • shrimps
— a la plancha	a la *plan*·cha	grilled prawns • shrimps
garbanzo m	gar·*ban*·tho	chickpea
gazpacho m	gath·*pa*·cho	cold soup made with garlic, tomato & vegetables
gazpachos m pl	gath·*pa*·chos	game dish with garlic & herbs
girasol m	*khee*·ra·sol	sunflower
granada f	gra·*na*·da	pomegranate
gratinada f	gra·tee·*na*·da	au gratin
guindilla f	gween·*dee*·lya	hot chilli pepper
guisantes m pl	gee·*san*·tes	peas

güisqui m	*gwee*·skee	whisky
hígado m	*ee*·ga·do	liver
haba f	*a*·ba	broad bean
hamburguesa f	am·boor·*ge*·sa	hamburger
harina f	a·*ree*·na	flour
helado m	e·*la*·do	ice cream
hervido/a m/f	er·*vee*·do/a	boiled
hierba buena f	*yer*·ba *bwe*·na	mint
higo m	*ee*·go	fig
hongo m	*on*·go	wild mushroom
horchata f	or·*cha*·ta	almond drink
horneado/a m/f	or·ne·*a*·do/a	baked
horno m	*or*·no	oven
hortalizas f pl	or·ta·*lee*·thas	vegetables
huevo m	*we*·vo	egg
huevos revueltos m pl	*we*·vos re·*vwel*·tos	scrambled eggs
infusión f	een·foo·*syon*	herbal tea
jabalí m	kha·ba·*lee*	wild boar
jamón m	kha·*mon*	ham
— dulce	*dool*·the	boiled ham
— serrano	se·*ra*·no	cured ham
jengibre m	khen·*khee*·bre	ginger
jerez m	khe·*reth*	sherry
judías f pl	khoo·*dee*·as	beans
— verdes	*ver*·des	green beans
— blancas	*blan*·kas	butter beans
langosta f	lan·*gos*·ta	spiny lobster
langostino m	lan·gos·*tee*·no	large prawn
lechuga f	le·*choo*·ga	lettuce
legumbre m	le·*goom*·bre	pulse
lengua f	*len*·gwa	tongue
lenguado m	len·*gwa*·do	sole
lentejas f pl	len·*te*·khas	lentils
lima f	*lee*·ma	lime

limón m	lee·*mon*	lemon
lomo m	*lo*·mo	pork loin • sausage
lomo con pimientos m	*lo*·mo kon pee·*myen*·tos	pork sausage with peppers
longaniza f	lon·ga·*nee*·tha	dark pork sausage
macarrones m pl	ma·ka·*ro*·nes	macaroni
magdalena f	mag·da·*le*·na	fairy cake (often dunked in coffee)
maíz f	ma·*eeth*	sweet corn
mandarina f	man·da·*ree*·na	tangerine
mango m	*man*·go	mango
manzana f	man·*tha*·na	apple
manzanilla f	man·tha·*nee*·lya	camomile • type of sherry • type of olive
marinado/a m/f	ma·ree·na·do/a	marinated
marisco m	ma·*rees*·ko	shellfish
martini m	mar·*tee*·nee	martini
mayonesa f	ma·yo·*ne*·sa	mayonnaise
mejillones m pl	me·khee·*lyo*·nes	mussels
— al vapor	al va·*por*	steamed mussels
melocotón m	mel·ko·*ton*	peach
melón m	me·*lon*	melon
membrillo m	mem·*bree*·lyo	quince
menta f	*men*·ta	mint
menú m *del dia*	me·*noo* del *dee*·a	set menu
merluza f	mer·*loo*·tha	hake
— a la plancha	a la *plan*·cha	fried hake
miel f	myel	honey
migas f pl	*mee*·gas	fried breadcrumb dish
mojama f	mo·*kha*·ma	cured tuna
montado m	mon·*ta*·do	tiny tapas sandwich
morcilla f	mor·*thee*·lya	blood sausage
muy hecho	mooy *e*·cho	well done
naranja f	na·*ran*·kha	orange
nata f	*na*·ta	cream

natillas f pl	na·*tee*·lyas	creamy milk dessert
nuez f	nweth	nut • walnut
orejón m	o·re·*khon*	dried apricot
ostras f pl	*os*·tras	oysters
paella f	pa·*e*·lya	rice & seafood dish (some varieties contain meat)
paloma f	pa·*lo*·ma	pigeon
pan m	pan	bread
parrilla f	pa·*ree*·lya	grilled
pasa f	*pa*·sa	raisin
pastas f pl	*pa*·stas	small cakes (available in a variety of flavours)
pastel m	pas·*tel*	cake • pastry
patatas f pl	pa·*ta*·tas	potatoes
— alioli	a·*lyo*·lee	garlic potatoes
— bravas	*bra*·vas	spicy, fried potatoes
patatas f pl *fritas*	pa·*ta*·tas *free*·tas	chips • French fries
patisería f	pa·tee·se·*ree*·a	cake shop
pato m	*pa*·to	duck
pavía f	pa·*vee*·a	battered
pavo m	*pa*·vo	turkey
pechuga f	pe·*choo*·ga	chicken breast
pepino m	pe·*pee*·no	cucumber
pera f	*pe*·ra	pear
perdiz f	per·*deeth*	partridge
peregrina f	pe·re·*gree*·na	scallop
pescadilla f	pes·ka·*dee*·lya	whiting
pescado m	pes·*ka*·do	fish
pescaíto m *frito*	pes·*kai*·to *free*·to	tiny fried fish
pez espada f	peth es·*pa*·da	swordfish
picadillo m	pee·ka·*dee*·lyo	minced meat
picante	pee·*kan*·te	spicy
pil pil m	peel peel	garlic sauce (sometimes with chilli)

pimienta f	pee·*myen*·ta	pepper
pimiento m	pee·*myen*·to	capsicum • pepper
pinchitos m pl	peen·*chee*·tos	Moroccan-style kebabs
pincho m	*peen*·cho	small tapas serving
piña f	*pee*·nya	pineapple
piñón m	pee·*nyon*	pine nut
pistacho m	pees·*ta*·cho	pistachio
plancha f	*plan*·cha	grill
plátano m	*pla*·ta·no	banana
platija f	pla·*tee*·kha	flounder
plato m	*pla*·to	plate
poco hecho	*po*·ko *e*·cho	rare
pollo m	*po*·lyo	chicken
postre m	*pos*·tre	dessert
potaje m	po·*ta*·khe	stew
primer plato m	pree·*mer pla* to	entrée • first course
puerro m	*pwe*·ro	leek
pulpo m	*pool*·po	octopus
— *a la gallega*	a la ga·*lye*·ga	octopus in sauce
queso m	*ke*·so	cheese
rabo m	*ra*·bo	tail
ración f	ra·*thyon*	small tapas plate or dish
rape m	*ra*·pe	monkfish
rebozado/a m/f	re·bo·*tha*·do/a	battered & fried
refrescos m pl	re·*fres*·kos	soft drinks
relleno/a m/f	re·*lye*·no/a	stuffed
remolacha f	re·mo·*la*·cha	beet
riñón m	ree·*nyon*	kidney
ron m	ron	rum
rosada f	ro·*sa*·da	ocean catfish • wolffish
sal f	sal	salt
salado/a m/f	sa·*la*·do/a	salted • salty
salchicha f	sal·*chee*·cha	fresh pork sausage
salchichón f	sal·chee·*chon*	peppery white sausage
salmón f	sal·*mon*	salmon

sandía f	san·*dee*·a	watermelon
sangría f	san·*gree*·a	*sangria* (red wine punch)
sardina f	sar·*dee*·na	sardine
seco/a m/f	*se*·ko/a	dry • dried
segundo plato m	se·*goon*·do *pla*·to	main course
sepia f	*se*·pya	cuttlefish
serrano m	se·*ra*·no	mountain-cured ham
sesos m pl	*se*·sos	brains
seta f	*se*·ta	wild mushroom
sidra f	*see*·dra	cider
sobrasada f	so·bra·*sa*·da	soft pork sausage
soja f	*so*·kha	soy
solomillo m	so·lo·*mee*·lyo	sirloin
sopa f	*so*·pa	soup
tapas f pl	*ta*·pas	bite-sized snacks
tarta f	*tar*·ta	cake
té m	te	tea
ternera f	ter·*ne*·ra	beef • veal
tinto	*teen*·to	red
tocino m	to·*thee*·no	bacon
tomate m	to·*ma*·te	tomato
torta f	*tor*·ta	round flat bun • cake
tortilla f	tor·*tee*·lya	omelette
— de patata	de pa·*ta*·ta	egg & potato omelette
— española	es·pa·*nyo*·la	potato omelette
tostada f	tos·*ta*·da	toast
trigo m	*tree*·go	wheat
trucha f	*troo*·cha	trout
trufa f	*troo*·fa	truffle
turrón m	too·*ron*	almond nougat
uva f	*oo*·va	grape
vaca f *(carne de)*	*va*·ka (*kar*·ne de)	beef
vegetal m	ve·khe·*tal*	vegetable
venera f	ve·*ne*·ra	scallop
verdura f	ver·*doo*·ra	green vegetable

vieira f	*vyey*·ra	scallop
vino m	*vee*·no	wine
— *de la casa*	de la *ka*·sa	house wine
zanahoria f	tha·na·*o*·rya	carrot
zarzuela f	thar·*thwe*·la	fish stew
zarzuela f *de marisco*	thar·*thwe*·la de ma·*rees*·ko	shellfish stew

Top tapas

Tapas are scrumptious cooked bar snacks, available pretty much around the clock at bars and some clubs. Take your pick from among these commonly found tasty morsels:

anchoas fritas a la catalana an·*cho*·as *free*·tas a la ka·ta·*la*·na
deep-fried anchovies

bacalao ba·ka·*low*
cod – usually salted and dried – prepared in various ways

boquerones bo·ke·*ro*·nes
fresh anchovies marinated in wine vinegar

callos *ka*·lyos
tripe – a popular Madrid tapa

caracoles ka·ra·*ko*·les
snails – sometimes served *a la riojana* (in a paprika sauce)

gambas al ajillo *gam*·bas al a·*khee*·lyo
garlic prawns • garlic shrimps

garbanzos con espinacas gar·*ban*·thos kon es·pee·*na*·kas
chickpeas with spinach

pulpo gallego *pool*·po ga·*lye*·go
boiled octopus in a spicy sauce

tortilla española tor·*tee*·lya es·pa·*nyo*·la
potato and onion omelette

SERVICES

Post office

I want to send a …	*Quisiera enviar …*	kee·*sye*·ra en·vee·*ar* …
fax	*un fax*	oon faks
parcel	*un paquete*	oon pa·*ke*·te
postcard	*una postal*	*oo*·na pos·*tal*
I want to buy (an) …	*Quisiera comprar …*	kee·*sye*·ra kom·*prar* …
envelope	*un sobre*	oon *so*·bre
some stamps	*sellos*	*se*·lyos
Please send it (to Australia) by …	*Por favor, mándelo (a Australia) por …*	por fa·*vor man*·de·lo (a ows·*tra*·lya) por …
airmail	*vía aérea*	*vee*·a a·*e*·re·a
express post	*correo urgente*	ko·*re*·o oor·*khen*·te
registered mail	*correo certificado*	ko·*re*·o ther·tee·fee·*ka*·do
surface mail	*vía terrestre*	*vee*·a te·*res*·tre

Bank

Where can I …?	*¿Dónde puedo …?*	*don*·de *pwe*·do …
I'd like to …	*Me gustaría …*	me goos·ta·*ree*·a …
cash a cheque	*cambiar un cheque*	kam·*byar* oon *che*·ke
change a travellers cheque	*cobrar un cheque de viajero*	ko·*brar* oon *che*·ke de vee·a·*khe*·ro
change money	*cambiar dinero*	kam·*byar* dee·*ne*·ro
get a cash advance	*obtener un adelanto*	ob·te·*ner* oon a·de·*lan*·to
withdraw money	*sacar dinero*	sa·*kar* dee·*ne*·ro

What time does the bank open?
¿A qué hora abre el banco? a ke *o*·ra *a*·bre el *ban*·ko

Can I arrange a transfer?
¿Puedo hacer una transferencia? *pwe*·do a·*ther* *oo*·na trans·fe·*ren*·thya

Where's the nearest foreign exchange office?
¿Dónde está la oficina de cambio más cercano? *don*·de es·*ta* la o·fee·*thee*·na de *kam*·byo mas ther·*ka*·no

Where's the nearest ATM?
¿Dónde está el cajero automatico más cercano? *don*·de es·*ta* el ka·*khe*·ro ow·to·*ma*·tee·ko o mas ther·*ka*·no

What's the ...?	*¿Cuál es ...?*	kwal es ...
exchange rate	*el tipo de cambio*	el *tee*·po de *kam*·byo
commission	*la comisión?*	la ko·mee·*syon*

Phone

What's your phone number?
¿Cuál es su/tu número de teléfono? pol/inf kwal es soo/too *noo*·me·ro de te·*le*·fo·no

Where's the nearest public phone?
¿Dónde hay una cabina telefónica? *don*·de ai *oo*·na ka·*bee*·na te·le·*fo*·nee·ka

I want to buy a phone card.
Quiero comprar una tarjeta telefónica. *kye*·ro kom·*prar* *oo*·na tar·*khe*·ta te·le·*fo*·nee·ka

I want to make a ... (to Singapore).	*Quiero hacer ... (a Singapur).*	*kye*·ro a·*ther* ... (a seen·ga·*poor*)
call	*una llamada*	*oo*·na lya·*ma*·da
reverse-charge/ collect call	*una llamada a cobro revertido*	*oo*·na lya·*ma*·da a *ko*·bro re·ver·*tee*·do

How much does … cost?	*¿Cuánto cuesta …?*	***kwan**·to **kwes**·ta …*
a (three)-minute call	*una llamada de (tres) minutos*	***oo**·na lya·**ma**·da de (tres) mee·**noo**·tos*
each extra minute	*cada minuto extra*	***ka**·da mee·**noo**·to **ek**·stra*

I want to speak for (three) minutes.
Quiero hablar por (tres) minutos. — **kye·ro a ·blar por (tres) mee·*noo*·tos**

The number is …
El número es … — **el *noo*·me·ro es …**

Mobile/cell phone

What are the rates?
¿Cuál es la tarifa? — **kwal es la ta·*ree*·fa**

(30c) per (30) seconds.
(Treinta centavos) por (treinta) segundos. — **(*treyn*·ta then·*ta*·vos) por (*treyn*·ta) se·*goon*·dos**

I'd like a/an …	*Quisiera …*	**kee·*sye*·ra …**
adaptor plug	*un adaptador*	**oon a·dap·ta·*dor***
charger for my phone	*un cargador para mi teléfono*	**oon kar·ga·*dor* *pa*·ra mee te·*le*·fo·no**
mobile/cell phone for hire	*un móvil para alquilar*	**oon *mo*·veel *pa*·ra al·kee·*lar***
prepaid phone card	*una tarjeta prepagada*	***oo*·na tar·*khe*·ta pre·pa·*ga*·da**
SIM card for your network	*una tarjeta SIM para su red*	***oo*·na tar·*khe*·ta seem *pa*·ra soo red**

Internet

Where's the local Internet café?

¿Dónde hay un cibercafé cercano?	*don*·de ai oon thee·ber·ka·*fe* ther·*ka*·no

How much per hour?

¿Cuánto cuesta por hora?	*kwan*·to *kwes*·ta por *o*·ra

How much per page?

¿Cuánto cuesta por página?	*kwan*·to *kwes*·ta por *pa*·khee·na

How much per CD?

¿Cuánto cuesta por cómpact?	*kwan*·to *kwes*·ta por *kom*·pakt

How do I log on?

¿Cómo entro al sistema?	*ko*·mo *en*·tro al sees·*te*·ma

It's crashed.

Se ha quedado colgado.	se a ke·*da*·do kol·*ga*·do

I've finished.

He terminado.	e ter·mee·*na*·do

I'd like to ...	*Quisiera ...*	kee·*sye*·ra ...
check my email	*revisar mi correo electrónico*	re·vee·*sar* mee ko·*re*·o e·lek·*tro*·nee·ko
get Internet access	*usar el Internet*	oo·*sar* el *een*·ter·net
use a printer	*usar una impresora*	oo·*sar oo*·na eem·pre·*so*·ra
use a scanner	*usar un escáner*	oo·*sar* oon es·*ka*·ner

Do you have ...?	*¿Tiene ...?*	*tye*·ne ...
Macs	*Apples*	*a*·pels
PCs	*PCs*	pe thes
a Zip drive	*unidad de Zip*	oo·nee·*da* de theep

GO

Directions

Where's (the Plaza Mayor)?
¿Dónde está (La Plaza Mayor)? — **don·de es·*ta* (la *pla*·tha ma·*yor*)**

I'm looking for (La Rambla).
Busco (La Rambla). — **boos·ko (la *ram*·bla)**

Which way is ...?
¿Por dónde se va a ...? — **por *don*·de se va a ...**

How far is it?
¿A cuánta distancia está? — **a *kwan*·ta dees·*tan*·thya es·*ta***

What's the address?
¿Cuál es la dirección? — **kwal es la dee·rek·*thyon***

Can you show me (on the map)?
¿Me lo puede indicar (en el mapa)? — **me lo *pwe*·de een·dee·*kar* (en el *ma*·pa)**

It's ...	*Está ...*	**es·*ta* ...**
behind ...	*detrás de ...*	**de·*tras* de ...**
beside ...	*al lado de ...*	**al *la*·do de**
far away	*lejos*	***le*·khos**
here	*aquí*	**a·*kee***
in front of ...	*enfrente de ...*	**en·*fren*·te de ...**
left	*por la izquierda*	**por la eeth·*kyer*·da**
near	*cerca*	***ther*·ka**
next to ...	*al lado de ...*	**al *la*·do de ...**
on the corner	*en la esquina*	**en la es·*kee*·na**
opposite ...	*frente a ...*	***fren*·te a ...**
right	*por la derecha*	**por la de·*re*·cha**
straight ahead	*todo recto*	***to*·do *rek*·to**
there	*ahí*	**a·*ee***

It's ...	*Está ...*	es·*ta* ...
... kilometres	*... kilómetros*	... kee·*lo*·me·tros
... metres	*... metros*	... *me*·tros
... minutes	*... minutos*	... mee·*noo*·tos
Turn ...	*Doble ...*	*do*·ble ...
at the corner	*en la esquina*	en la es·*kee*·na
at the traffic lights	*en el semáforo*	en el se·*ma*·fo·ro
left/right	*a la izquierda/ derecha*	a la eeth·*kyer*·da/ de·*re*·cha
by bus	*por autobús*	por ow·to·*boos*
by metro	*en metro*	en me·*tro*
by taxi	*por taxi*	por *tak*·see
by train	*por tren*	por tren
on foot	*a pie*	a pye
north	*nor* m	nor
south	*sur* m	soor
east	*este* m	*es*·te
west	*oeste* m	*wes*·te

Getting around

What time does the ... leave?	*¿A qué hora sale el ...?*	a ke *o*·ra *sa*·le el ...
boat	*barco*	*bar*·ko
bus (city)	*autobús*	ow·to·*boos*
bus (intercity)	*autocar*	ow·to·*kar*
plane	*avión*	a·*vyon*
train	*tren*	tren
tram	*tranvia*	tran·*vee*·a

What time's the ... (bus)?	*¿A qué hora es el ... (autobús)?*	a ke *o*·ra es el ... (ow·to·*boos)*
first	*primer*	pree·*mer*
last	*último*	*ool*·tee·mo
next	*próximo*	*prok*·see·mo

I want to get off ...	*Quiero bajarme ...*	*kye*·ro ba·*khar*·me ...
at (Seville)	*en (Sevilla)*	en (se·*vee*·lya)
here	*aquí*	a·*kee*

How many stops to ...?
¿Cuántas paradas hay hasta ...? — *kwan*·tas pa·*ra*·das ai *as*·ta ...

Can you tell me when we get to ...?
¿Me podría decir cuándo lleguemos a ...? — me po·*dree*·a de·*theer* *kwan*·do lye·*ge*·mos a ...

Is this seat free?
¿Está libre este asiento? — es·*ta lee*·bre *es*·te a·*syen*·to

That's my seat.
Ése es mi asiento. — *e*·se es mee a·*syen*·to

GO

Tickets & luggage

Where can I buy a ticket?
¿Dónde puedo comprar un billete? — *don*·de *pwe*·do kom·*prar* oon bee·*lye*·te

Do I need to book?
¿Tengo que reservar? — *ten*·go ke re·ser·*var*

How long does the trip take?
¿Cuánto se tarda? — *kwan*·to se *tar*·da

A one-way ticket to (Cádiz).
Un billete sencillo a (Cádiz). — oon bee·*lye*·te sen·*thee*·lyo a (*ka*·deeth)

I'd like to ...	*Me gustaría ...*	**me goos·ta·*ree*·a ...**
my ticket.	*mi billete.*	**mee bee·*lye*·te**
cancel	*cancelar*	**kan·the·*lar***
change	*cambiar*	**kam·*byar***
confirm	*confirmar*	**kon·feer·*mar***

One ... ticket, please.	*Un billete ..., por favor.*	**oon bee·*lye*·te ... por fa·*vor***
1st-class	*de primera clase*	**de pree·*me*·ra *kla*·se**
2nd-class	*de segunda clase*	**de se·*goon*·da *kla*·se**
child's	*infantil*	**een·fan·*teel***
return	*de ida y vuelta*	**de *ee*·da ee *vwel*·ta**
student's	*de estudiante*	**de es·too·*dyan*·te**

I'd like a/an ... seat.	*Quisiera un asiento ...*	**kee·*sye*·ra oon a·*syen*·to ...**
aisle	*de pasillo*	**de pa·*see*·lyo**
nonsmoking	*de no fumadores*	**de no foo·ma·*do*·res**
smoking	*de fumadores*	**de foo·ma·*do*·res**
window	*junto a la ventana*	***khoon*·to a la ven·*ta*·na**

Is there (a) ...?	*¿Hay ...?*	**ai ...**
air-conditioning	*aire acondicionado*	***ai*·re a·kon·dee·thyo·*na*·do**
blanket	*una manta*	***oo*·na *man*·ta**
toilet	*servicios*	**ser·*vee*·thyos**
video	*vídeo*	***vee*·de·o**

Is it a direct route?
¿Es un viaje directo? **es oon *vya*·khe dee·*rek*·to**

What time do I have to check in?
¿A qué hora tengo que facturar mi equipaje? **a ke *o*·ra *ten*·go ke fak·too·*rar* mee e·kee·*pa*·khe**

GO

Can I get a stand-by ticket?
¿Puede ponerme en la lista de espera? — *pwe*·de po·*ner*·me en la *lees*·ta de es·*pe*·ra

I'd like a luggage locker.
Quisiera un casillero de consigna. — kee·*sye*·ra oon ka·see·*lye*·ro de kon·*seeg*·na

Can I have some coins/tokens?
¿Me podría dar monedas/fichas? — me po·*dree*·a dar mo·*ne*·das/*fee*·chas

Where's the baggage claim?
¿Dónde está la recogida de equipages? — *don*·de es·*ta* la re·ko·*khee*·da de e·kee·*pa*·khes

GO

My luggage has been ...	*Mis maletas han sido ...*	mees ma·*le*·tas an *see*·do ...
damaged	*dañadas*	da·*nya*·das
lost	*perdidas*	per·*dee*·das
stolen	*robadas*	ro·*ba*·das

Bus, metro, taxi & train

Which city/intercity bus goes to ...?
¿Qué autobús/autocar va a ...? — ke ow·to·*boos*/ow·to·*kar* va a ...

Is this the bus to ...?
¿Es el autobús para ...? — es el ow·to·*boos* *pa*·ra ...

What station is this?
¿Cuál es esta estación? — kwal es *es*·ta es·ta·*thyon*

What's the next station?
¿Cuál es la próxima estación? — kwal es la *prok*·see·ma es·ta·*thyon*

Does this train stop at (Aranjuez)?
¿Para el tren en (Aranjuez)? *pa*·ra el tren en (a·*ran*·khweth)

Do I need to change trains?
¿Tengo que cambiar de tren? *ten*·go ke kam·*byar* de tren

How many stops to (the museum)?
¿Cuántas paradas hay hasta (el museo)? *kwan*·tas pa·*ra*·das ai *as*·ta (el moo·*se*·o)

Which carriage is . . . ?	*¿Cuál es el coche . . . ?*	kwal es el *ko*·che . . .
for (Valencia)	*para (Valencia)*	*pa*·ra (va·*len*·thya)
1st class	*de primera clase*	de pree·*me*·ra *kla*·se
for dining	*comedor*	ko·me·*dor*

I'd like a taxi . . .	*Quisiera un taxi . . .*	kee·*sye*·ra oon *tak*·see . . .
at (9am)	*a (las nueve de la mañana)*	a (las *nwe*·ve de la ma·*nya*·na)
now	*ahora*	a·*o*·ra
tomorrow	*mañana*	ma·*nya*·na

Is this taxi free?
¿Está libre este taxi? es·*ta lee*·bre *es*·te *tak*·see

Please put the meter on.
Por favor, ponga el taxímetro. por fa·*vor pon*·ga el tak·*see*·me·tro

How much is it to . . . ?
¿Cuánto cuesta ir a . . . ? *kwan*·to *kwes*·ta eer a . . .

Please take me to (this address).
Por favor, lléveme a (esta dirección). por fa·*vor lye*·ve·me a (*es*·ta dee·rek·*thyon*)

Please ...	*Por favor ...*	por fa·*vor* ...
slow down	*vaya más despacio*	*va*·ya mas des·*pa*·thyo
wait here	*espere aquí*	es·*pe*·re a·*kee*

Stop ...	*Pare ...*	*pa*·re ...
at the corner	*en la esquina*	en la es·*kee*·na
here	*aquí*	a·*kee*

Car & motorbike hire

I'd like to hire a/an ...	*Quisiera alquilar ...*	kee·*sye*·ra al·*kee*·lar ...
(small/large) car	*un coche (grande/ pequeño)*	oon *ko*·che (*gran*·de/ pe·*ke*·nyo)
motorbike	*una moto*	*oo*·na *mo*·to

with ...	*con ...*	kon ...
air-conditioning	*aire acondicionado*	*ai*·re a·kon·dee·thyo·*na*·do
antifreeze	*anticongelante*	an·tee·kon·khe·*lan*·te
snow chains	*cadenas de nieve*	ka·*de*·nas de *nye*·ve

How much for ... hire?	*¿Cuánto cuesta el alquiler por ...?*	*kwan*·to *kwes*·ta el al·*kee*·ler por ...
daily	*día*	*dee*·a
hourly	*hora*	*o*·ra
weekly	*semana*	se·*ma*·na

Does that include insurance/mileage?
¿Incluye el seguro/ kilometraje? — een·*kloo*·ye el se·*goo*·ro/ kee·lo·me·*tra*·khe

Is this the road to ...?

¿Se va a ... por esta carretera?	se va a ... por *es*·ta ka·re·*te*·ra

Where's a petrol station?

¿Dónde hay una gasolinera?	*don*·de ai *oo*·na ga·so·lee·*ne*·ra

(How long) Can I park here?

¿(Por cuánto tiempo) Puedo aparcar aquí?	(por *kwan*·to tyem·po) *pwe*·do a·par·*kar* a·*kee*

What's the ... speed limit?	*¿Cuál es el límite de velocidad ...?*	kwal es el *lee*·mee·te de ve·lo·thee·*da* ...
city	*en la ciudad*	en la theew·*da*
country	*en el campo*	en el *kam*·po

GO

Road signs

Acceso	ak·*the*·so	Entrance
Aparcamiento	a·par·ka·*myen*·to	Parking
Ceda el Paso	*the*·da el *pa*·so	Give Way
Desvío	des·*vee*·o	Detour
Dirección Única	dee·rek·*thyon oo*·nee·ka	One Way
Frene	*fre*·ne	Slow Down
Peaje	pe·*a*·khe	Toll
Peligro	pe·*lee*·gro	Danger
Prohibido Aparcar	pro·ee·*bee*·do a·par·*kar*	No Parking
Prohibido el Paso	pro·ee·*bee*·do el *pa*·so	No Entry
Stop	es·*top*	Stop
Vía de Acceso	*vee*·a de ak·*the*·so	Freeway Entrance

SLEEP

Finding accommodation

Where's a ...?	*¿Dónde hay ...?*	***don**·de ai ...*
bed and breakfast	*una pensión con desayuno*	**oo**·na pen·**syon** kon de·sa·**yoo**·no
camping ground	*terreno de cámping*	te·**re**·no de **kam**·peen
guesthouse	*una pensión*	**oo**·na pen·**syon**
hotel	*un hotel*	oon o·**tel**
youth hostel	*un albergue juvenil*	oon al·**ber**·ge khoo·ve·**neel**

Can you recommend somewhere ...?	*¿Puede recomendar algún sitio ...?*	**pwe**·de re·ko·men·**dar** al·**goon see**·tee·o ...
cheap	*barato*	ba·**ra**·to
luxurious	*de lujo*	de **loo**·kho
nearby	*cercano*	ther·**ka**·no
nice	*agradable*	a·gra·**da**·ble
romantic	*romántico*	ro·**man**·tee·ko

What's the address?
¿Cuál es la dirección? — kwal es la dee·rek·**thyon**

Booking ahead & checking in

I'd like to book a room, please.
Quisiera reservar una habitación. — kee·**sye**·ra re·ser·**var** **oo**·na a·bee·ta·**thyon**

I have a reservation.
He hecho una reserva. — e **e**·cho **oo**·na re·**ser**·va

My name's ...
Me llamo ... — me **lya**·mo ...

Do you have a … room?	*¿Tiene una habitación …?*	*tye*·ne *oo*·na a·bee·ta·*thyon* …
double	*doble*	*do*·ble
single	*individual*	een·dee·vee·*dwal*
twin	*con dos camas*	kon dos *ka*·mas

How much is it per …?	*¿Cuánto cuesta por …?*	*kwan*·to *kwes*·ta por …
night	*noche*	*no*·che
person	*persona*	per·*so*·na
week	*semana*	se·*ma*·na

For (three) nights.
Por (tres) noches. — por (tres) *no*·ches

From (July 2) to (July 6).
Desde (el dos de julio) hasta (el seis de julio). — *des*·de (el dos de *khoo*·lyo) *as*·ta (el seys de *khoo*·lyo)

Can I see it?
¿Puedo verla? — *pwe*·do *ver*·la

It's fine. I'll take it.
Vale, la alquilo. — *va*·le la al·*kee*·lo

Do I need to pay upfront?
¿Necesito pagar por adelantado? — ne·the·*see*·to pa·*gar* por a·de·lan·*ta*·do

Do you accept …?	*¿Aceptan …?*	a·*thep*·tan …
credit cards	*tarjetas de crédito*	tar·*khe*·tas de *kre*·dee·to
debit cards	*tarjetas de débito*	tar·*khe*·tas de *de*·bee·to
travellers cheques	*cheques de viajero*	*che*·kes de vya·*khe*·ro

SLEEP

Requests & queries

When/Where is breakfast served?
¿Cuándo/Dónde se sirve el desayuno? — *kwan*·do/*don*·de se *seer*·ve el de·sa·*yoo*·no

Please wake me at (seven).
Por favor, despiértame a (las siete). — por fa·*vor* des·*pyer*·te·me a (las *sye*·te)

Can I use the . . . ?	*¿Puedo usar . . . ?*	*pwe*·do oo·*sar* . . .
kitchen	*la cocina*	la ko·*thee*·na
laundry	*el lavadero*	el la·va·*de*·ro
telephone	*el teléfono*	el te·*le*·fo·no

Is there a/an . . . ?	*¿Hay . . . ?*	ai . . .
elevator	*ascensor*	as·then·*sor*
laundry service	*servicio de lavandería*	ser·*vee*·thyo de la·van·de·*ree*·a
safe	*una caja fuerte*	*oo*·na *ka*·kha *fwer*·te

Do you . . . here?	*¿Aquí . . . ?*	a·*kee* . . .
arrange tours	*organizan recorridos*	or·ga·*nee*·than re·ko·*ree*·dos
change money	*cambian dinero*	*kam*·byan dee·*ne*·ro

It's too . . .	*Es demasiado . . .*	es de·ma·*sya*·do . . .
cold	*fría*	*free*·a
dark	*oscura*	os·*koo*·ra
expensive	*cara*	*ka*·ra
light	*clara*	*kla*·ra
noisy	*ruidosa*	rwee·*do*·sa
small	*pequeña*	pe·*ke*·nya

The … doesn't work.	*No funciona …*	no foon·*thyo*·na …
air-conditioning	*el aire acondicionado*	el *ai*·re a·kon·dee·thyo·*na*·do
fan	*el ventilador*	el ven·tee·la·*dor*
toilet	*el retrete*	el re·*tre*·te
window	*la ventana*	la ven·*ta*·na

Can I get another …?	*¿Puede darme otra …?*	*pwe*·de *dar*·me *o*·tra …
This … isn't clean.	*Ésta … no está limpia.*	*es*·ta … no es·*ta leem*·pya
blanket	*manta*	*man*·ta
pillow	*almohada*	al·*mwa*·da
pillowcase	*funda de almohada*	*foon*·da de al·*mwa*·da
sheet	*sábana*	*sa*·ba·na
towel	*toalla*	*twa*·lya

Checking out

What time is check out?
¿A qué hora hay que dejar libre la habitación? — a ke *o*·ra ai ke de·*khar lee*·bre la a·bee·ta·*thyon*

Can I leave my bags here?
¿Puedo dejar las maletas aquí? — *pwe*·do de·*khar* las ma·*le*·tas a·*kee*

Could I have …, please?	*¿Me puede dar …, por favor?*	me *pwe*·de dar … por fa·*vor*
my deposit	*mi depósito*	mee de·*po*·see·to
my passport	*mi pasaporte*	mee pa·sa·*por*·te
my valuables	*mis objetos de valor*	mees ob·*khe*·tos de va·*lor*

I'll be back …	*Volveré …*	vol·ve·*re* …
in (three) days	*en (tres) días*	en (tres) *dee*·as
on (Tuesday)	*el (martes)*	el (*mar*·tes)

WORK
Introductions

Where's the . . . ?	*¿Dónde está . . . ?*	*don*·de es·*ta* . . .
business centre	*el servicio secretarial*	el ser·*vee*·thyo se·kre·*ta*·ryal
conference	*el congreso*	el kon·*gre*·so
I'm attending a . . .	*Asisto a . . .*	a·*sees*·to a . . .
conference	*un congreso*	oon kon·*gre*·so
course	*un curso*	oon *koor*·so
meeting	*una reunión*	*oo*·na re·oo·*nyon*
trade fair	*una feria de muestras*	*oo*·na *fe*·rya de *mwes*·tras
I'm with . . .	*Estoy con . . .*	es·*toy* kon . . .
(the UN)	*(el ONU)*	(el o en oo)
my colleague(s)	*mi(s) colega(s)*	mee(s) ko·*le*·ga(s)
(two) others	*otros (dos)*	*ot*·ros (dos)

Here's my business card.
Aquí tiene mi tarjeta de visita. — a·*kee tye*·ne mee tar·*khe*·ta de vee·*see*·ta

Let me introduce my colleague.
¿Puedo presentarle a mi compañero/a? m/f — *pwe*·do pre·sen·*tar*·le a mee kom·pa·*nye*·ro/a

I'm alone.
Estoy solo/a. m/f — es·*toy so*·lo/a

I'm staying at . . ., room . . .
Me estoy alojando en . . ., la habitación . . . — me es·*toy* a·lo·*khan*·do en . . ., la a·bee·ta·*thyon* . . .

I'm here for (two) days/weeks.
Estoy aquí por (dos) días/semanas. — es·*toy* a·*kee* por (dos) *dee*·as/se·*ma*·nas

Business needs

I have an appointment with …
Tengo una cita con … — *ten*·go *oo*·na *thee*·ta kon …

I'm expecting …	*Estoy esperando …*	es·*toy* es·pe·*ran*·do …
a call	*una llamada*	*oo*·na lya·*ma*·da
a fax	*un fax*	oon faks
I need …	*Necesito …*	ne·se·*thee*·to …
a connection to the Net	*una conexión al Internet*	*oo*·na ko·nek·*syon* al een·ter·*net*
an interpreter	*un/una intérprete* m&f	oon/*oo*·na een·*ter*·pre·te
to make photocopies	*hacer fotocopias*	a·*ther* fo·to·*ko*·pyas
to send an email/fax	*enviar un email/fax*	en·*vyar* oon *ee*·mayl/faks
laser pointer	*puntero* m *láser*	poon·*te*·ro *la*·ser
overhead projector	*retroproyector* m *de transparencias*	re·tro·pro·yek·*tor* de tran·spa·*ren*·thyas
whiteboard	*pizarra* f *blanca*	pee·*tha*·ra *blan*·ka

After the deal

That went very well.
Eso fue muy bien. — *e*·so fwe mooy byen

Shall we go for a drink/meal?
¿Vamos a tomar/comer algo? — *va*·mos a to·*mar*/ko·*mer al*·go

It's on me.
Invito yo. — een·*vee*·to yo

HELP

Emergencies

Help!	*¡Socorro!*	so·*ko*·ro
Stop!	*¡Pare!*	*pa*·re
Go away!	*¡Váyase!*	*va*·ya·se
Thief!	*¡Ladrón!*	lad·*ron*
Fire!	*¡Fuego!*	*fwe*·go
Watch out!	*¡Cuidado!*	kwee·*da*·do

It's an emergency.
Es una emergencia. es *oo*·na e·mer·*khen*·thya

Call the police!
¡Llame a la policía! *lya*·me a la po·lee·*thee*·a

Call a doctor!
¡Llame a un médico! *lya*·me a oon *me*·dee·ko

Call an ambulance!
¡Llame a una ambulancia! *lya*·me a *oo*·na am·boo·*lan*·thya

Could you help me, please?
¿Me puede ayudar, por favor? me *pwe*·de a·yoo·*dar* por fa·*vor*

I have to use the telephone.
Necesito usar el teléfono. ne·the·*see*·to oo·*sar* el te·*le*·fo·no

I'm lost.
Estoy perdido/a. m/f es·*toy* per·*dee*·do/a

Where are the toilets?
¿Dónde están los servicios? *don*·de es·*tan* los ser·*vee*·thyos

Leave me alone!
¡Déjame en paz! *de*·kha·me en path

Police

Where's the police station?		
¿Dónde está la comisaria?		*don*·de es·*ta* la ko·mee·sa·*ree*·a
I want to report an offence.		
Quiero denunciar un delito.		*kye*·ro de·noon·*thyar* oon de·*lee*·to
I've been assaulted.		
He sido asaltado/a. m/f		e *see*·do a·sal·*ta*·do/a
I've been robbed.		
Me han robado.		me an ro·*ba*·do
I've been raped.		
He sido violado/a. m/f		e *see*·do vee·o·*la*·do/a
My ... was stolen.		
Mi ... fue robado/a. m/f		mee ... fwe ro·*ba*·do/a
My ... were stolen.		
Mis ... fueron robados/as. m/f		mees ... fwe·*ron* ro·*ba*·dos/as

I've lost my ...	*He perdido ...*	e per·*dee*·do ...
backpack	*mi mochila*	mee mo·*chee*·la
bags	*mis maletas*	mees ma·*le*·tas
credit card	*mi tarjeta de crédito*	mee tar·*khe*·ta de *kre*·dee·to
handbag	*mi bolso*	mee *bol*·so
money	*mi dinero*	mee dee·*ne*·ro
passport	*mi pasaporte*	mee pa·sa·*por*·te
wallet	*mi cartera*	mee kar·*te*·ra

I want to contact my embassy/consulate.	
Quiero ponerme en contacto con mi embajada/consulado.	*kye*·ro po·*ner*·me en kon·*tak*·to kon mee em·ba·*kha*·da/kon·soo·*la*·do
I have a prescription for this drug.	
Tengo receta para esta droga.	*ten*·go re·*the*·ta *pa*·ra *es*·ta *dro*·ga

Health

Where's the nearest ...?	*¿Dónde está ... más cercano/a?* m/f	*don*·de es·*ta* ... mas ther·*ka*·no/a
chemist	*la farmacia* f	la far·*ma*·thya
dentist	*el dentista* m	el den·*tees*·ta
doctor	*el médico* m	el *me*·dee·ko
hospital	*el hospital* m	el os·pee·*tal*
medical centre	*el consultorio* m	el kon·sool·*to*·ryo
optometrist	*el oculista* m	el o·koo·*lees*·ta

I need a doctor (who speaks English).
Necesito un médico (que hable inglés). — ne·the·*see*·to oon *me*·dee·ko (ke *a*·ble een·*gles*)

Could I see a female doctor?
¿Puede examinarme una médica? — *pwe*·de ek·sa·mee·*nar*·me *oo*·na *me*·dee·ka

Can the doctor come here?
¿Puede visitarme el médico? — *pwe*·de vee·see·*tar*·me el *me*·dee·ko

I've run out of my medication.
Se me terminaron los medicamentos. — se me ter·mee·*na*·ron los me·dee·ka·*men*·tos

My prescription is ...
Mi receta es ... — mee re·se·ta es ...

I've been vaccinated against ...	*Estoy vacunado/a contra ...* m/f	es·*toy* va·koo·*na*·do/a *kon*·tra ...
... fever	*la fiebre ...*	la *fye*·bre ...
hepatitis A/B/C	*la hepatitis A/B/C*	la e·pa·*tee*·tees a/be/the
tetanus	*el tétano*	el *te*·ta·no
typhoid	*la tifus*	la *tee*·foos

Symptoms, conditions & allergies

I'm sick.
Estoy enfermo/a. m/f — es·*toy* en·*fer*·mo/a

It hurts here.
Me duele aquí. — me *dwe*·le a·*kee*

I've been injured.
He sido herido/a. m/f — e *see*·do e·*ree*·do/a

I've been vomiting.
He estado vomitando. — e es·*ta*·do vo·mee·*tan*·do

I feel …	*Me siento …*	me *syen*·to …
better	*mejor*	me·*khor*
dizzy	*mareado/a* m/f	ma·re·*a*·do
nauseous	*con nauseas*	kon *now*·se·as
shivery	*destemplado/a* m/f	des·tem·*pla*·do/a
worse	*peor*	pe·*or*

For more symptoms & conditions, see the dictionary in **LOOK UP**.

Do I need a prescription for …?
¿Necesito receta para …? — ne·the·*see*·to re·*the*·ta *pa*·ra …

I have a prescription.
Tengo receta médica. — *ten*·go re·*the*·ta *me*·dee·ka

How many times a day?
¿Cuántas veces al día? — *kwan*·tas *ve*·thes al *dee*·a

I have …
Tengo … — *ten*·go …

I've recently had …
Hace poco he tenido … — *a*·the *po*·ko e te·*nee*·do …

I'm on regular medication for ...

Estoy bajo medicación para ...	es·*toy ba*·kho me·dee·ka·*thyon pa*·ra ...

asthma	*asma* m	*as*·ma
allergy	*alergia* f	a·ler·*khee*·a
bronchitis	*bronquitis* m	bron·*kee*·tees
cold	*resfriado* m	res·free·*a*·do
cough	*tos* f	tos
diabetes	*diabetes* m	dee·a·*be*·tes
diarrhoea	*diarrea* f	dee·a·*re*·a
fever	*fiebre* f	*fye*·bre
headache	*dolor* m *de cabeza*	do·lor de ka·*be*·tha
heart condition	*condición* f *cardíaca*	kon·dee·*thyon* kar·*dya*·ka
infection	*infección* f	een·fek·*thyon*
sprain	*torcedura* f	tor·the·*doo*·ra

I'm allergic to ...	*Soy alérgico/a ...* m/f	soy a·*ler*·khee·ko/a ...
antibiotics	*a los antibióticos*	a los an·tee·*byo*·tee·kos
anti-inflammatories	*a los anti-inflamatorios*	a los an·tee·een·fla·ma·*to*·ryos
aspirin	*a la aspirina*	a la as·pee·*ree*·na
bees	*a las abejas*	a las a·*be*·khas
codeine	*a la codeina*	a la ko·de·*ee*·na
nuts	*a las nueces*	a las *nwe*·thes
peanuts	*a los cacahuetes*	a los ka·ka·*we*·tes
penicillin	*a la penicilina*	a la pe·nee·thee·*lee*·na
pollen	*al polen*	al *po*·len

I have a skin allergy.

Tengo una alergia en la piel.	*ten*·go *oo*·na a·*ler*·khya en la pyel

For more food-related allergies, see **EAT & DRINK,** page 32.

Numbers

0	*cero*	*the*·ro
1	*uno*	*oo*·no
2	*dos*	dos
3	*tres*	tres
4	*cuatro*	*kwa*·tro
5	*cinco*	*theen*·ko
6	*seis*	seys
7	*siete*	*sye*·te
8	*ocho*	*o*·cho
9	*nueve*	*nwe*·ve
10	*diez*	dyeth
11	*once*	*on*·the
12	*doce*	*do*·the
13	*trece*	*tre*·the
14	*catorce*	ka·*tor*·the
15	*quince*	*keen*·the
16	*dieciséis*	dye·thee·*seys*
17	*diecisiete*	dye·thee·*sye*·te
18	*dieciocho*	dye·thee·*o*·cho
19	*diecinueve*	dye·thee·*nwe*·ve
20	*veinte*	*veyn*·te
21	*veintiuno*	veyn·tee·*oo*·no
22	*veintidós*	veyn·tee·*dos*
30	*treinta*	*treyn*·ta
40	*cuarenta*	kwa·*ren*·ta
50	*cincuenta*	theen·*kwen*·ta
60	*sesenta*	se·*sen*·ta
70	*setenta*	se·*ten*·ta
80	*ochenta*	o·*chen*·ta
90	*noventa*	no·*ven*·ta
100	*cien*	thyen
101	*ciento uno*	*thyen*·to *oo*·no
102	*ciento dos*	*thyen*·to dos
500	*quinientos*	kee·*nyen*·tos
1,000	*mil*	meel
1,000,000	*un millón*	oon mee·*lyon*

Colours

dark ...	*... oscuro*	... o·*skoo*·ro
light ...	*... claro*	... *kla*·ro
black	*negro/a*	*ne*·gro/a
blue	*azul*	a·*thool*
brown	*marrón*	ma·*ron*
green	*verde*	*ver*·de
grey	*gris*	grees
orange	*naranja*	na·*ran*·kha
pink	*rosa*	*ro*·sa
purple	*lila*	*lee*·la
red	*rojo/a*	*ro*·kho/a
white	*blanco/a*	*blan*·ko/a
yellow	*amarillo/a*	a·ma·*ree*·lyo/a

Time & dates

What time is it?	*¿Qué hora es?*	ke *o*·ra es
It's (one) o'clock.	*Es (la una).*	es (la *oo*·na)
It's (ten) o'clock.	*Son (las diez).*	son (las dyeth)
Quarter past one.	*Es la una y cuarto.*	es la *oo*·na ee *kwar*·to
Twenty past one.	*Es la una y veinte.*	es la *oo*·na ee *veyn*·te
Half past one.	*Es la una y media.*	es la *oo*·na ee *me*·dya
Twenty to one.	*Es la una menos veinte.*	es la *oo*·na *me*·nos *veyn*·te
Quarter to one.	*Es la una menos cuarto.*	es la *oo*·na *me*·nos *kwar*·to
At what time?	*¿A qué hora?*	a ke o·ra
At …	*A …*	a …
am	*de la mañana*	de la ma·*nya*·na
pm	*de la tarde*	de la *tar*·de

Monday	*lunes*	*loo*·nes
Tuesday	*martes*	*mar*·tes
Wednesday	*miércoles*	*myer*·ko·les
Thursday	*jueves*	*khwe*·ves
Friday	*viernes*	*vyer*·nes
Saturday	*sábado*	*sa*·ba·do
Sunday	*domingo*	do·*meen*·go

January	*enero*	e·*ne*·ro
February	*febrero*	fe·*bre*·ro
March	*marzo*	*mar*·tho
April	*abril*	a·*breel*
May	*mayo*	*ma*·yo
June	*junio*	*khoo*·nyo
July	*julio*	*khoo*·lyo
August	*agosto*	a·*gos*·to
September	*septiembre*	sep·*tyem*·bre
October	*octubre*	ok·*too*·bre
November	*noviembre*	no·*vyem*·bre
December	*diciembre*	dee·*thyem*·bre

spring	*primavera* f	pree·ma·*ve*·ra
summer	*verano* m	ve·*ra*·no
autumn	*otoño* m	o·*to*·nyo
winter	*invierno* m	een·*vyer*·no

What date?
¿Qué día? — ke *dee*·a

What date is it today?
¿Qué día es hoy? — ke *dee*·a es oy

It's (18 October).
Es (el dieciocho de octubre). — es (el dye·thee·*o*·cho de ok·*too*·bre)

last …		
month	*el mes pasado*	el mes pa·*sa*·do
night	*anoche*	a·*no*·che
week	*la semana pasada*	la se·*ma*·na pa·*sa*·da
year	*el año pasado*	el *a*·nyo pa·*sa*·do
next …	*… que viene*	… ke *vye*·ne
month	*el mes*	el mes
week	*la semana*	la se·*ma*·na
year	*el año*	el *a*·nyo
since (May)	*desde (mayo)*	*des*·de (*ma*·yo)
tomorrow …	*mañana por la …*	ma·*nya*·na por la …
afternoon	*tarde*	*tar*·de
evening	*noche*	*no*·che
morning	*mañana*	ma·*nya*·na
yesterday …	*ayer por la …*	a·*yer* por la …
afternoon	*tarde*	*tar*·de
evening	*noche*	*no*·che
morning	*mañana*	ma·*nya*·na

English–Spanish dictionary

Nouns in this dictionary have their gender indicated by m (masculine) or f (feminine). If it's a plural noun, you'll also see pl.
Where no gender is marked the word is either an adjective or a verb, with adjectives first.

A

aboard *a bordo* a *bor*·do
accident *accidente* m ak·thee·*den*·te
accommodation *alojamiento* m a·lo·kha·*myen*·to
across *a través* a tra·*ves*
adaptor *adaptador* m a·dap·ta·*dor*
address *dirección* f dee·rek·*thyon*
admission price *precio* m *de entrada* *pre*·thyo de en·*tra*·da
after *después de* des·*pwes* de
aftershave *bálsamo de aftershave* *bal*·sa·mo de *af*·ter·sha·eev
again *otra vez* o·tra veth
air-conditioned *con aire acondicionado* kon *ai*·re a·kon·dee·thyo·*na*·do
airline *aerolínea* f ay·ro·*lee*·nya
airplane *avión* m a·*vyon*
airport *aeropuerto* m ay·ro·*pwer*·to
airport tax *tasa* f *del aeropuerto* *ta*·sa del ay·ro·*pwer*·to
alarm clock *despertador* m des·per·ta·*dor*
alcohol *alcohol* m al·*kol*
all *todo* *to*·do
allergy *alergia* f a·*ler*·khya
alone *solo/a* m/f *so*·lo/a
ambulance *ambulancia* m am·boo·*lan*·thya
and *y* ee
ankle *tobillo* m to·*bee*·lyo
antibiotics *antibióticos* m pl an·tee·*byo*·tee·kos
antique *antigüedad* f an·tee·gwe·*da*
antiseptic *antiséptico* m an·tee·*sep*·tee·ko
appointment *cita* f *thee*·ta
architect *arquitecto/a* m/f ar·kee·*tek*·to/a
architecture *arquitectura* f ar·kee·tek·*too*·ra
arm *brazo* m *bra*·tho
arrivals *llegadas* f pl lye·*ga*·das
arrive *llegar* lye·*gar*
art *arte* m *ar*·te
art gallery *museo* m *de arte* moo·*se*·o de *ar*·te
artist *artista* m&f ar·*tees*·ta
ashtray *cenicero* m the·nee·*the*·ro
aspirin *aspirina* f as·pee·*ree*·na
assault *asalto* m a·*sal*·to
aunt *tía* f *tee*·a
Australia *Australia* f ow·*stra*·lya
automatic teller machine *cajero* m *automático* ka·*khe*·ro ow·to·*ma*·tee·ko

B

B&W (film) *blanco y negro* *blan*·ko ee *ne*·gro
baby *bebé* m be·*be*
baby food *comida* f *de bebé* ko·*mee*·da de be·*be*
babysitter *canguros* m kan·*goo*·ros
back (of body) *espalda* f es·*pal*·da
backpack *mochila* f mo·*chee*·la
bacon *tocino* m to·*thee*·no
bad *malo/a* m/f *ma*·lo/a
bag *bolso* m *bol*·so
baggage *equipaje* m e·kee·*pa*·khe
baggage allowance *límite* m *de equipaje* *lee*·mee·te de e·kee·*pa*·khe
baggage claim *recogida* f *de equipajes* re·ko·*khee*·da de e·kee·*pa*·khes
bakery *panadería* f pa·na·de·*ree*·a
band *grupo* m *groo*·po
bandage *vendaje* m ven·*da*·khe
band-aids *tiritas* f pl tee·*ree*·tas
bank *banco* m *ban*·ko
bank account *cuenta* f *bancaria* *kwen*·ta ban·*ka*·rya
banknotes *billetes* m pl *(de banco)* bee·*lye*·tes (de *ban*·ko)

bar (venue) *bar* m bar
bar (with music) *pub* m poob
bath *bañera* f ba·*nye*·ra
bathroom *baño* m *ba*·nyo
battery *pila* f *pee*·la
beach *playa* f *pla*·ya
beautiful *hermoso/a* m/f er·*mo*·so/a
beauty salon *salón* m *de belleza* sa·*lon* de be·*lye*·tha
bed *cama* f *ka*·ma
bedding *ropa* f *de cama* *ro*·pa de *ka*·ma
bedroom *habitación* f a·bee·ta·*thyon*
beer *cerveza* f ther·*ve*·tha
before *antes* *an*·tes
begin *comenzar* ko·men·*thar*
behind *detrás de* de·*tras* de
best *lo mejor* lo me·*khor*
better *mejor* me·*khor*
bicycle *bicicleta* f bee·thee·*kle*·ta
big *grande* *gran*·de
bill *cuenta* f *kwen*·ta
birthday *cumpleaños* m koom·ple·*a*·nyos
black *negro/a* m/f *ne*·gro/a
blanket *manta* f *man*·ta
blister *ampolla* f am·*po*·lya
blocked *atascado/a* m/f a·tas·*ka*·do/a
blood *sangre* f *san*·gre
blood group *grupo* m *sanguíneo* *groo*·po san·*gee*·neo
blue *azul* a·*thool*
board (ship, etc) *embarcarse* em·bar·*kar*·se
boarding house *pensión* f pen·*syon*
boarding pass *tarjeta* f *de embarque* tar·*khe*·ta de em·*bar*·ke
book *libro* m *lee*·bro
book (make a reservation) *reservar* re·ser·*var*
booked out *lleno/a* m/f *lye*·no/a
bookshop *librería* f lee·bre·*ree*·a
boots *botas* f pl *bo*·tas
border *frontera* f fron·*te*·ra
boring *aburrido/a* m/f a·boo·*ree*·do/a
both *los/las dos* m/f pl los/las dos
bottle *botella* f bo·*te*·lya
bottle opener *abrebotellas* m a·bre·bo·*te*·lyas
bowl *bol* m bol
box *caja* f *ka*·kha
boy *chico* m *chee*·ko
boyfriend *novio* m *no*·vyo
bra *sujetador* m soo·khe·ta·*dor*
brakes *frenos* m pl *fre*·nos
bread *pan* m pan
breakfast *desayuno* m des·a·*yoo*·no
bridge *puente* m *pwen*·te
briefcase *maletín* m ma·le·*teen*
brochure *folleto* m fo·*lye*·to
broken *roto/a* m/f *ro*·to/a
brother *hermano* m er·*ma*·no
brown *marrón* ma·*ron*
buffet *buffet* m boo·*fe*
building *edificio* m e·dee·*fee*·thyo
bull *toro* m *to*·ro
bullfight *corrida* f ko·*ree*·da
bullring *plaza* f *de toros* *pla*·tha de *to*·ros
burn *quemadura* f ke·ma·*doo*·ra
bus (city) *autobús* m ow·to·*boos*
bus (intercity) *autocar* m ow·to·*kar*
bus station (city) *estación* f *de autobuses* es·ta·*thyon* de ow·to·*boo*·ses
bus station (intercity) *estación* f *de autocares* es·ta·*thyon* de ow·to·*ka*·res
bus stop *parada* f *de autobús* pa·*ra*·da de ow·to·*boos*
business *negocios* m pl ne·*go*·thyos
business class *clase* f *preferente* *kla*·se pre·fe·*ren*·te
business person *comerciante* m&f ko·mer·*thyan*·te
busker *artista callejero/a* m/f ar·*tees*·ta ka·lye·*khe*·ro/a
busy *ocupado/a* m/f o·koo·*pa*·do/a
but *pero* *pe*·ro
butcher's shop *carnicería* f kar·nee·the·*ree*·a
buttons *botónes* m pl bo·*to*·nes
buy *comprar* kom·*prar*

LOOK UP

C

café *cafe* m ka·*fe*
cake shop *pastelería* f pas·te·le·*ree*·a
calculator *calculadora* f kal·koo·la·*do*·ra
camera *cámara* f *(fotográfica)* *ka*·ma·ra (fo·to·*gra*·fee·ka)
camera shop *tienda* f *de fotografía* *tyen*·da de fo·to·gra·*fee*·a
campsite *cámping* m *kam*·peen
can *lata* f *la*·ta
can opener *abrelatas* m a·bre·*la*·tas
Canada *Canadá* f ka·na·*da*
cancel *cancelar* kan·the·*lar*
car *coche* m *ko*·che
car hire *alquiler* m *de coche* al·kee·*ler* de *ko*·che
car owner's title *papeles* m pl *del coche* pa·*pe*·les del *ko*·che
car registration *matrícula* f ma·*tree*·koo·la
carpark *aparcamiento* m a·par·ka·*myen*·to
cash *dinero* m *en efectivo* dee·*ne*·ro en e·fek·*tee*·vo
cash (a cheque) *cambiar (un cheque)* kam·*byar* (oon *che*·ke)
cash register *caja* f *registradora* *ka*·kha re·khees·tra·*do*·ra
cashier *caja* f *ka*·kha
cassette *casete* m ka·*se*·te
castle *castillo* m kas·*tee*·lyo
cathedral *catedral* f ka·te·*dral*
Catholic *católico/a* m/f ka·*to*·lee·ko/a
CD *cómpact* m *kom*·pakt
cemetery *cementerio* m the·men·*te*·ryo
centimetre *centímetro* m then·*tee*·me·tro
centre *centro* m *then*·tro
chair *silla* f *see*·lya
champagne *champán* m cham·*pan*
change *cambio* m *kam*·byo
change *cambiar* kam·*byar*
changing rooms *vestuarios* m pl ves·*twa*·ryos
cheap *barato/a* m/f ba·*ra*·to/a
check (bank) *cheque* m *che*·ke
check-in *facturación* f *de equipajes* fak·too·ra·*thyon* de e·kee·*pa*·khes
cheese *queso* m *ke*·so
chef *cocinero* m ko·thee·*ne*·ro
chemist (pharmacist) *farmacéutico/a* m/f far·ma·the·*oo*·tee·ko/a
chemist (shop) *farmacia* f far·*ma*·thya
chest *pecho* m *pe*·cho
chicken *pollo* m *po*·lyo
child *niño/a* m/f *nee*·nyo/a
child seat *asiento* m *de seguridad para bebés* a·*syen*·to de se·goo·ree·*da* *pa*·ra be·*bes*
childminding service *guardería* f gwar·de·*ree*·a
children *hijos* m pl *ee*·khos
chilli *guindilla* f geen·*dee*·lya
chocolate *chocolate* m cho·ko·*la*·te
Christian name *nombre* m *de pila* *nom*·bre de *pee*·la
Christmas *Navidad* f na·vee·*da*
church *iglesia* f ee·*gle*·sya
cigar *cigarro* m thee·*ga*·ro
cigarette *cigarillo* m thee·ga·*ree*·lyo
cigarette lighter *mechero* m me·*che*·ro
cinema *cine* m *thee*·ne
circus *circo* m *theer*·ko
citizenship *ciudadanía* f theew·da·da·*nee*·a
city *ciudad* f theew·*da*
city centre *centro* m *de la ciudad* *then*·tro de la theew·*da*
classical *clásico/a* m/f *kla*·see·ko/a
clean *limpio/a* m/f *leem*·pyo/a
cleaning *limpieza* f leem·*pye*·tha
client *cliente* m&f klee·*en*·te
cloakroom *guardarropa* m gwar·da·*ro*·pa
close *cerrar* the·*rar*
closed *cerrado/a* m/f the·*ra*·do/a
clothing *ropa* f *ro*·pa
clothing store *tienda* f *de ropa* *tyen*·da de *ro*·pa
coast *costa* f *kos*·ta
coffee *café* m ka·*fe*

coins *monedas* f pl mo·*ne*·das
cold (illness) *resfriado* m res·free·*a*·do
cold (temperature) *frío/a* m/f *free*·o/a
colleague *colega* m&f ko·*le*·ga
collect call *llamada* f *a cobro revertido* lya·*ma*·da a *ko*·bro re·ver·*tee*·do
colour *color* m ko·*lor*
comb *peine* m *pey*·ne
come *venir* ve·*neer*
come (arrive) *llegar* lye·*gar*
comfortable *cómodo/a* m/f *ko*·mo·do/a
companion *compañero/a* m/f kom·pa·*nye*·ro/a
company *compañía* f kom·pa·*nyee*·a
complain *quejarse* ke·*khar*·se
computer *ordenador* m or·de·na·*dor*
concert *concierto* m kon·*thyer*·to
conditioner *acondicionador* m a·kon·dee·thyo·na·*dor*
condoms *condones* m pl kon·*do*·nes
confession *confesión* f kon·fe·*syon*
confirm *confirmar* kon·feer·*mar*
connection *conexión* f ko·ne·*ksyon*
constipation *estreñimiento* m es·tre·nyee·*myen*·to
consulate *consulado* m kon·soo·*la*·do
contact lenses *lentes* m pl *de contacto* *len*·tes de kon·*tak*·to
convenience store *negocio* m *de artículos básicos* ne·*go*·thyo de ar·*tee*·koo·los *ba*·see·kos
cook *cocinero* m ko·thee·*ne*·ro
cook *cocinar* ko·thee·*nar*
corkscrew *sacacorchos* m sa·ka·*kor*·chos
cost *costar* kos·*tar*
cotton *algodón* m al·go·*don*
cotton balls *bolas* f pl *de algodón* *bo*·las de al·go·*don*
cough *tos* f tos
cough medicine *jarabe* m kha·*ra*·be
countryside *campo* m *kam*·po
court (tennis) *pista* f *pees*·ta
cous cous *cus cus* m koos koos
cover charge *precio* m *del cubierto* *pre*·thyo del koo·*byer*·to
crafts *artesanía* f ar·te·sa·*nee*·a
cream *crema* *kre*·ma
crèche *guardería* f gwar·de·*ree*·a
credit card *tarjeta* f *de crédito* tar·*khe*·ta de *kre*·dee·to
cup *taza* f *ta*·tha
currency exchange *cambio* m *(de dinero)* *kam*·byo (de dee·*ne*·ro)
current (electricity) *corriente* f ko·*ryen*·te
customs *aduana* f a·*dwa*·na
cut *cortar* kor·*tar*
cutlery *cubiertos* m pl koo·*byer*·tos

D

daily *diariamente* dya·rya·*men*·te
dance *bailar* bai·*lar*
dancing *baile* m *bai*·le
dangerous *peligroso/a* m/f pe·lee·*gro*·so/a
dark *oscuro/a* m/f os·*koo*·ro/a
date *citarse* thee·*tar*·se
date (time) *fecha* f *fe*·cha
date of birth *fecha* f *de nacimiento* *fe*·cha de na·thee·*myen*·to
daughter *hija* f *ee*·kha
dawn *alba* f *al*·ba
day *día* m *dee*·a
day after tomorrow *pasado mañana* pa·*sa*·do ma·*nya*·na
day before yesterday *anteayer* an·te·a·*yer*
delay *demora* f de·*mo*·ra
deliver *entregar* en·tre·*gar*
dental floss *hilo* m *dental* *ee*·lo den·*tal*
dentist *dentista* m&f den·*tees*·ta
deodorant *desodorante* m de·so·do·*ran*·te
depart *salir de* sa·*leer* de
department store *grandes almacenes* m pl *gran*·de al·ma·*then*·es
departure *salida* f sa·*lee*·da
deposit *depósito* m de·*po*·see·to
destination *destino* m des·*tee*·no
diabetes *diabetes* f dee·a·*be*·tes

diaper *pañal* m pa·*nyal*
diaphragm *diafragma* m dee·a·*frag*·ma
diarrhoea *diarrea* f dee·a·*re*·a
diary *agenda* f a·*khen*·da
dictionary *diccionario* m deek·thyo·*na*·ryo
different *diferente* m&f dee·fe·*ren*·te
dining car *vagón* m *restaurante* va·*gon* res·tow·*ran*·te
dinner *cena* f *the*·na
direct *directo/a* m/f dee·*rek*·to/a
direct-dial *marcar directo* mar·kar dee·*rek*·to
dirty *sucio/a* m/f *soo*·thyo/a
disabled *minusválido/a* m/f mee·noos·*va*·lee·do/a
discount *descuento* m des·*kwen*·to
disk *disco* m *dees*·ko
doctor *médico/a* m/f *me*·dee·ko/a
documentary *documental* m do·koo·men·*tal*
dog *perro/a* m/f *pe*·ro/a
dollar *dólar* m *do*·lar
dope *droga* f *dro*·ga
double bed *cama* f *de matrimonio* *ka*·ma de ma·tree·*mo*·nyo
double room *habitación* f *doble* a·bee·ta·*thyon* *do*·ble
down *abajo* a·*ba*·kho
dress *vestido* m ves·*tee*·do
drink *bebida* f be·*bee*·da
drink *beber* be·*ber*
drive *conducir* kon·doo·*theer*
drivers licence *carnet* m *de conducir* kar·*ne* de kon·doo·*theer*
drug *droga* f *dro*·ga
drunk *borracho/a* m/f bo·*ra*·cho/a
dry *secar* se·*kar*
duck *pato* m *pa*·to
dummy (pacifier) *chupete* m choo·*pe*·te

E

each *cada* *ka*·da
ear *oreja* f o·*re*·kha
early *temprano* tem·*pra*·no
earplugs *tapones* m pl *para los oídos* ta·*po*·nes *pa*·ra los o·*ee*·dos
earrings *pendientes* m pl pen·*dyen*·tes
east *este* *es*·te
Easter *Pascua* f *pas*·kwa
eat *comer* ko·*mer*
economy class *clase* f *turística* *kla*·se too·*rees*·tee·ka
electrical store *tienda* f *de productos eléctricos* *tyen*·da de pro·*dook*·tos e·*lek*·tree·kos
electricity *electricidad* f e·lek·tree·thee·*da*
elevator *ascensor* m as·then·*sor*
email *correo* m *electrónico* ko·*re*·o e·lek·*tro*·nee·ko
embassy *embajada* f em·ba·*kha*·da
emergency *emergencia* f e·mer·*khen*·thya
empty *vacío/a* m/f va·*thee*·o/a
end *acabar* a·ka·*bar*
engagement *compromiso* m kom·pro·*mee*·so
engine *motor* m mo·*tor*
engineer *ingeniero/a* m/f een·khe·*nye*·ro/a
engineering *ingeniería* f een·khe·nye·*ree*·a
England *Inglaterra* f een·gla·*te*·ra
English *inglés* m een·*gles*
enough *suficiente* m/f soo·fee·*thyen*·te
enter *entrar* en·*trar*
entertainment guide *guía* f *del ocio* *gee*·a del *o*·thyo
envelope *sobre* m *so*·bre
escalator *escaleras* f pl *mecánicas* es·ka·*le*·ras me·*ka*·nee·kas
euro *euro* m *e*·oo·ro
Europe *Europa* f e·oo·*ro*·pa
evening *noche* f *no*·che
everything *todo* *to*·do
exchange *cambio* m *kam*·byo
exchange (money) *cambiar* kam·*byar*
exchange rate *tipo* m *de cambio* *tee*·po de *kam*·byo
exhibition *exposición* f eks·po·see·*thyon*
exit *salida* f sa·*lee*·da

expensive *caro/a* m/f ka·ro/a
express mail *correo* m *urgente* ko·re·o oor·khen·te
eye *ojo* m o·kho

F

face *cara* f ka·ra
fall *caída* f ka·ee·da
family *familia* f fa·mee·lya
family name *apellido* m a·pe·lyee·do
fan (electric) *ventilador* m ven·tee·la·dor
fan (hand held) *abanico* m a·ba·nee·ko
far *lejos* le·khos
fast *rápido/a* m/f ra·pee·do/a
fat *gordo/a* m/f gor·do/a
father *padre* m pa·dre
father-in-law *suegro* m swe·gro
faulty *defectuoso/a* m/f de·fek·too·o·so/a
feel *sentir* sen·teer
feelings *sentimientos* m pl sen·tee·myen·tos
festival (celebration) *fiesta* f fyes·ta
festival (art, music) *festival* m fes·tee·val
fever *fiebre* f fye·bre
fiancé *prometido* m pro·me·tee·do
fiancée *prometida* f pro·me·tee·da
film *película* f pe·lee·koo·la
film speed *sensibilidad* f sen·see·bee·lee·da
fine *multa* f mool·ta
finger *dedo* m de·do
first *primero/a* m/f pree·me·ro/a
first-aid kit *maletín* m *de primeros auxilios* ma·le·teen de pree·me·ros ow·ksee·lyos
first-class *de primera clase* de pree·me·ra kla·se
fish (live) *pez* m peth
fish (food) *pescado* m pes·ka·do
fish shop *pescadería* f pes·ka·de·ree·a
fishing *pesca* f pes·ka
flashlight *linterna* f leen·ter·na
floor *suelo* m swe·lo
flower *flor* f flor
fly *volar* vo·lar
food *comida* f ko·mee·da
foot *pie* m pye
football *fútbol* m foot·bol
footpath *acera* f a·the·ra
foreign *extranjero/a* m/f eks·tran·khe·ro/a
forest *bosque* m bos·ke
forever *para siempre* pa·ra syem·pre
fork *tenedor* m te·ne·dor
fortnight *quincena* f keen·the·na
fragile *frágil* fra·kheel
free (not bound) *libre* lee·bre
free (of charge) *gratis* gra·tees
friend *amigo/a* m/f a·mee·go/a
frozen foods *productos* m pl *congelados* pro·dook·tos kon·khe·la·dos
fruit *fruta* f froo·ta
fry *freír* fre·eer
frying pan *sartén* f sar·ten
full *lleno/a* m/f lye·no/a
funny *gracioso/a* m/f gra·thyo·so/a
furniture *muebles* m pl mwe·bles
future *futuro* m foo·too·ro

G

gasoline *gasolina* f ga·so·lee·na
gay *gay* ge
Germany *Alemania* f a·le·ma·nya
gift *regalo* m re·ga·lo
gig *bolo* m bo·lo
girl *chica* f chee·ka
girlfriend *novia* f no·vya
glass (drinking) *vaso* m va·so
glass (material) *vidrio* m vee·dree·o
glasses *gafas* f pl ga·fas
gloves *guantes* m pl gwan·tes
go *ir* eer
go out with *salir con* sa·leer kon
go shopping *ir de compras* eer de kom·pras
golf course *campo* m *de golf* kam·po de golf
good *bueno/a* m/f bwe·no/a
gram *gramo* m gra·mo
grandchild *nieto/a* m/f nye·to/a
grandfather *abuelo* m a·bwe·lo
grandmother *abuela* f a·bwe·la
gray *gris* grees
great *fantástico/a* m/f fan·tas·tee·ko/a

green *verde* ver·de
grey *gris* grees
grocery *tienda* f *de comestibles* tyen·da de ko·mes·tee·bles
grow *crecer* kre·ther
guide (person) *guía* m&f gee·a
guidebook *guía* f gee·a
guided tour *recorrido* m *guiado* re·ko·ree·do gee·a·do

H

hairdresser *peluquero/a* m/f pe·loo·ke·ro/a
half *medio/a* m/f me·dyo/a
hand *mano* f ma·no
handbag *bolso* m bol·so
handicrafts *artesanía* f ar·te·sa·nee·a
handmade *hecho a mano* e·cho a ma·no
handsome *hermoso/a* m/f er·mo·so/a
happy *feliz* fe·leeth
hard *duro/a* m/f doo·ro/a
hat *sombrero* m som·bre·ro
have *tener* te·ner
hay fever *alergia* f *al polen* a·ler·khya al po·len
he *él* el
head *cabeza* f ka·be·tha
headache *dolor* m *de cabeza* do·lor de ka·be·tha
headlights *faros* m pl fa·ros
heart *corazón* m ko·ra·thon
heart condition *condición* f *cardíaca* kon·dee·thyon kar·dee·a·ka
heat *calor* m ka·lor
heater *estufa* f es·too·fa
heavy *pesado/a* m/f pe·sa·do/a
help *ayudar* a·yoo·dar
her *su* soo
here *aquí* a·kee
high *alto/a* m/f al·to/a
hike *ir de excursión* eer de eks·koor·syon
hiking *excursionismo* m eks·koor·syo·nees·mo
hire *alquilar* al·kee·lar
his *su* soo
hitchhike *hacer dedo* a·ther de·do
holidays *vacaciones* f pl va·ka·thyo·nes
homosexual *homosexual* m&f o·mo·se·kswal
honeymoon *luna* f *de miel* loo·na de myel
hospital *hospital* m os·pee·tal
hot *caliente* ka·lyen·te
hotel *hotel* m o·tel
hungry *tener hambre* te·ner am·bre
husband *marido* m ma·ree·do

I

I *yo* yo
ice *hielo* m ye·lo
ice cream *helado* m e·la·do
identification *identificación* f ee·den·tee·fee·ka·thyon
identification card *carnet* m *de identidad* kar·net de ee·den·tee·da
ill *enfermo/a* m/f en·fer·mo/a
important *importante* eem·por·tan·te
included *incluido* een·kloo·ee·do
indigestion *indigestion* f een·dee·khes·tyon
influenza *gripe* f gree·pe
injection *inyección* f een·yek·thyon
injury *herida* f e·ree·da
insurance *seguro* m se·goo·ro
intermission *descanso* m des·kan·so
Internet m *Internet* een·ter·net
Internet café *cibercafe* m thee·ber·ka·fe
interpreter *intérprete* m&f een·ter·pre·te
Ireland *Irlanda* f eer·lan·da
iron *plancha* f plan·cha
island *isla* f ees·la
IT *informática* f een·for·ma·tee·ka
itch *picazón* f pee·ka·thon
itinerary *itinerario* m ee·tee·ne·ra·ryo

J

jacket *chaqueta* f cha·ke·ta
jeans *vaqueros* m pl va·ke·ros

jet lag *jet lag* m dyet lag
jewellery shop *joyería* f kho·ye·*ree*·a
job *trabajo* m tra·*ba*·kho
journalist *periodista* m&f pe·ryo·*dees*·ta
jumper (sweater) *jersey* m *kher*·sey

K

key *llave* f *lya*·ve
kilogram *kilogramo* m *kee*·lo·gram·o
kilometre *kilómetro* m kee·*lo*·me·tro
kind *amable* a·*ma*·ble
kitchen *cocina* f ko·*thee*·na
knee *rodilla* f ro·*dee*·lya
knife *cuchillo* m koo·*chee*·lyo

L

lake *lago* m *la*·go
languages *idiomas* m pl ee·*dyo*·mas
laptop *ordenador* m *portátil* or·de·na·*dor* por·*ta*·teel
late *tarde* *tar*·de
laundrette *lavandería* f la·van·de·*ree*·a
laundry *lavadero* m la·va·*de*·ro
law *ley* f ley
lawyer *abogado/a* m/f a·bo·*ga*·do/a
leather *cuero* m *kwe*·ro
left luggage *consigna* f kon·*seeg*·na
leg *pierna* f *pyer*·na
lens *objetivo* m ob·khe·*tee*·vo
lesbian *lesbiana* f les·bee·*a*·na
less *menos* *me*·nos
letter *carta* f *kar*·ta
library *biblioteca* f bee·blyo·*te*·ka
lifejacket *chaleco* m *salvavidas* cha·*le*·ko sal·va·*vee*·das
lift *ascensor* m as·then·*sor*
light *luz* f looth
light (colour) *claro* *cla*·ro
light (weight) *leve* *le*·ve
lighter *encendedor* m en·then·de·*dor*
like *gustar(le)* goos·*tar*(le)
line *línea* f *lee*·ne·a
lipstick *pintalabios* m *peen*·ta *la*·byos
liquor store *bodega* f bo·*de*·ga
listen *escuchar* es·koo·*char*
local *de cercanías* de ther·ka·*nee*·as
lock *cerradura* f the·ra·*doo*·ra
lock *cerrar* the·*rar*
locked *cerrado/a* m/f *con llave* the·*ra*·do/a kon *lya*·ve
long *largo/a* m/f *lar*·go/a
lost *perdido/a* m/f per·*dee*·do/a
lost property office *oficina* f *de objetos perdidos* o·fee·*thee*·na de ob·*khe*·tos per·*dee*·dos
love *querer* ke·*rer*
lubricant *lubricante* m loo·bree·*kan*·te
luggage *equipaje* m e·kee·*pa*·khe
lunch *almuerzo* m al·*mwer*·tho
luxury *lujo* m *loo*·kho

M

mail *correo* m ko·*re*·o
mailbox *buzón* m boo·*thon*
make-up *maquillaje* m ma·kee·*lya*·khe
man *hombre* m *om*·bre
manager *gerente* m&f *khe*·ren·te
map *mapa* m *ma*·pa
market *mercado* m mer·*ka*·do
marry *casarse* ka·*sar*·se
massage *masaje* m ma·*sa*·khe
masseur/masseuse *masajista* m&f ma·sa·*khees*·ta
match *partido* m par·*tee*·do
matches *cerillas* f pl the·*ree*·lyas
mattress *colchón* m kol·*chon*
measles *sarampión* m sa·ram·*pyon*
meat *carne* f *kar*·ne
medicine *medicina* f me·dee·*thee*·na
menu *menú* m me·*noo*
message *mensaje* m men·*sa*·khe
metre *metro* m *me*·tro
metro station *estación* f *de metro* es·ta·*thyon* de *me*·tro
microwave *microondas* m mee·kro·*on*·das
midnight *medianoche* f me·dya·*no*·che

milk *leche* f *le*·che
millimetre *milímetro* m mee·*lee*·me·tro
mineral water *agua* f *mineral* *a*·gwa mee·ne·*ral*
minute *minuto* m mee·*noo*·to
mirror *espejo* m es·*pe*·kho
mobile phone *teléfono* m *móvil* te·*le*·fo·no *mo*·veel
modem *módem* m *mo*·dem
moisturiser *crema* f *hidratante* *kre*·ma ee·dra·*tan*·te
money *dinero* m dee·*ne*·ro
month *mes* m mes
morning (6am–1pm) *mañana* f ma·*nya*·na
mother *madre* f *ma*·dre
mother-in-law *suegra* f *swe*·gra
motorcycle *motocicleta* f mo·to·thee·*kle*·ta
motorway *autovia* f ow·to·*vee*·a
mountain *montaña* f mon·*ta*·nya
mouth *boca* f *bo*·ka
movie *película* f pe·*lee*·koo·la
museum *museo* m moo·*se*·o
music *música* f *moo*·see·ka
musician *músico/a* m/f *moo*·see·ko/a
my *mi* mee

N

nail clippers *cortauñas* m pl kor·ta·*oo*·nyas
name *nombre* m *nom*·bre
name (given) *nombre* m *de pila* *nom*·bre de *pee*·la
napkin *servilleta* f ser·vee·*lye*·ta
nappy *pañal* m pa·*nyal*
nausea *náusea* f *now*·se·a
near *cerca* *ther*·ka
nearby *cerca* *ther*·ka
nearest *más cercano/a* m/f mas ther·*ka*·no/a
necklace *collar* m ko·*lyar*
needle (sewing) *aguja* f a·*goo*·kha
Netherlands *Holanda* f o·*lan*·da
new *nuevo/a* m/f *nwe*·vo/a
New Year *Año Nuevo* m *a*·nyo *nwe*·vo
New Year's Eve *Nochevieja* f no·che·*vye*·kha
New Zealand *Nueva Zelanda* f *nwe*·va the·*lan*·da

news *noticias* f pl no·*tee*·thyas
newsagency *quiosco* m *kyos*·ko
newspaper *periódico* m pe·*ryo*·dee·ko
next (month) *el próximo (mes)* el *prok*·see·mo (mes)
night *noche* f *no*·che
no *no* no
noisy *ruidoso/a* m/f rwee·*do*·so/a
nonsmoking *no fumadores* no foo·ma·*do*·res
north *norte* m *nor*·te
nose *nariz* f na·*reeth*
notebook *cuaderno* m kwa·*der*·no
nothing *nada* *na*·da
now *ahora* a·*o*·ra
number *número* m *noo*·me·ro
nurse *enfermero/a* m/f en·fer·*me*·ro/a

O

off (food) *pasado/a* m/f pa·*sa*·do/a
oil *aceite* m a·*they*·te
old *viejo/a* m/f *vye*·kho/a
olive oil *aceite* m *de oliva* a·*they*·te de o·*lee*·va
on *en* en
once *vez* f veth
one-way ticket *billete* m *sencillo* bee·*lye*·te sen·*thee*·lyo
open *abierto/a* m/f a·*byer*·to/a
open *abrir* a·*breer*
opening hours *horas* f pl *de abrir* *o*·ras de a·*breer*
orange (colour) *naranja* na·*ran*·kha
other *otro/a* m/f *o*·tro/a
our *nuestro/a* m/f *nwes*·tro/a
outside *exterior* m eks·te·*ryor*

P

pacifier (dummy) *chupete* m choo·*pe*·te
package *paquete* m pa·*ke*·te
packet *paquete* m pa·*ke*·te
padlock *candado* m kan·*da*·do

LOOK UP

pain *dolor* m do·*lor*
painful *doloroso/a* m/f do·lo·*ro*·so/a
painkillers *analgésicos* m pl a·nal·*khe*·see·kos
painter *pintor/pintora* m/f peen·*tor*/ peen·*to*·ra
painting *pintura* f peen·*too*·ra
palace *palacio* m pa·*la*·thyo
pants *pantalones* m pl pan·ta·*lo*·nes
panty liners *salvaeslips* m pl sal·va·e·*sleeps*
pantyhose *medias* f pl *me*·dyas
paper *papel* m pa·*pel*
paperwork *trabajo* m *administrativo* tra·*ba*·kho ad·mee·nees·tra·*tee*·vo
parents *padres* m pl *pa*·dres
park *parque* m *par*·ke
park (car) *estacionar* es·ta·thyo·*nar*
party *fiesta* f *fyes*·ta
passenger *pasajero/a* m/f pa·sa·*khe*·ro
passport *pasaporte* m pa·sa·*por*·te
passport number *número* m *de pasaporte noo*·me·ro de pa·sa·*por*·te
past *pasado* m pa·*sa*·do
path *sendero* m sen·*de*·ro
pay *pagar* pa·*gar*
payment *pago* m *pa*·go
pen *bolígrafo* m bo·*lee*·gra·fo
pencil *lápiz* m *la*·peeth
penis *pene* m *pe*·ne
penknife *navaja* f na·*va*·kha
pensioner *pensionista* m&f pen·syo·*nees*·ta
per (day) *por (día)* por (*dee*·a)
perfume *perfume* m per·*foo*·me
petrol *gasolina* f ga·so·*lee*·na
pharmacy *farmacia* f far·*ma*·thya
phone book *guía* f *telefónica gee*·a te·le·*fo*·nee·ka
phone box *cabina* f *telefónica* ka·*bee*·na te·le·*fo*·nee·ka
phone card *tarjeta* f *de teléfono* tar·*khe*·ta de te·*le*·fo·no
photograph *foto* f *fo*·to
photograph *sacar fotos* sa·*kar fo*·tos
photographer *fotógrafo/a* m/f fo·*to*·gra·fo/a
photography *fotografía* f fo·to·gra·*fee*·a
phrasebook *libro* m *de frases lee*·bro de *fra*·ses
picnic *comida* f *en el campo* ko·*mee*·da en el *kam*·po
pill *pastilla* f pas·*tee*·lya
pillow *almohada* f al·*mwa*·da
pillowcase *funda* f *de almohada foon*·da de al·*mwa*·da
pink *rosa ro*·sa
pistachio *pistacho* m pees·*ta*·cho
plane *avión* m a·*vyon*
plate *plato* m *pla*·to
platform *plataforma* f pla·ta·*for*·ma
play *obra* f *o*·bra
plug *tapar* ta·*par*
point *apuntar* a·poon·*tar*
police *policía* f po·lee·*thee*·a
police station *comisaría* f ko·mee·sa·*ree*·a
pool (swimming) *piscina* f pees·*thee*·na
post code *código postal* m *ko*·dee·go pos·*tal*
post office *correos* m ko·*re*·os
postage *franqueo* m fran·*ke*·o
postcard *postal* f pos·*tal*
poster *póster* m *pos*·ter
pound (money) *libra* f *lee*·bra
pregnant *embarazada* f em·ba·ra·*tha*·da
premenstrual tension *tensión* f *premenstrual* ten·*syon* pre·mens·*trwal*
price *precio* m *pre*·thyo
private *privado/a* m/f pree·*va*·do/a
pub *pub* m poob
public telephone *teléfono* m *público* te·*le*·fo·no *poo*·blee·ko
public toilet *servicios* m pl ser·*vee*·thyos
pull *tirar* tee·*rar*
purple *lila lee*·la

Q

quiet *tranquilidad* f tran·kee·lee·*da*

LOOK UP

R

railway station *estación* f *de tren* es·ta·*thyon* de tren
rain *lluvia* f *lyoo*·vya
raincoat *impermeable* m eem·per·me·*a*·ble
rare *raro/a* m/f *ra*·ro/a
razor *afeitadora* f a·fey·ta·*do*·ra
razor blades *cuchillas* f pl *de afeitar* koo·*chee*·lyas de a·fey·*tar*
receipt *recibo* m re·*thee*·bo
recommend *recomendar* re·ko·men·*dar*
red *rojo/a* m/f *ro*·kho/a
refrigerator *nevera* f ne·*ve*·ra • *frigerífico* m free·ge·*ree*·fee·ko
refund *reembolsar* re·em·bol·*sar*
registered mail *correo* m *certificado* ko·*re*·o ther·tee·fee·*ka*·do
remote control *mando* m *a distancia* *man*·do a dees·*tan*·thya
rent *alquilar* al·kee·*lar*
repair *reparar* re·pa·*rar*
reservation *reserva* f re·*ser*·va
restaurant *restaurante* m res·tow·*ran*·te
return *volver* vol·*ver*
return ticket *billete* m *de ida y vuelta* bee·*lye*·te de *ee*·da ee *vwel*·ta
right (correct) *correcto/a* m/f ko·*rek*·to/a
right (not left) *derecha* de·*re*·cha
ring *llamar por telefono* lya·*mar* por te·*le*·fo·no
road *carretera* f ka·re·*te*·ra
rock (music) *rock* m rok
romantic *romántico/a* m/f ro·*man*·tee·ko/a
room *habitación* f a·bee·ta·*thyon*
room number *número* m *de la habitación* *noo*·me·ro de la a·bee·ta·*thyon*
ruins *ruinas* f pl *rwee*·nas

S

safe *caja* f *fuerte* *ka*·kha *fwer*·te
safe sex *sexo* m *seguro* *se*·kso se·*goo*·ro
sanitary napkins *compresas* f pl kom·*pre*·sas
scarf *bufanda* f boo·*fan*·da
school *escuela* f es·*kwe*·la
science *ciencias* f pl *thyen*·thyas
scientist *científico/a* m/f thyen·*tee*·fee·ko/a
scissors *tijeras* f pl tee·*khe*·ras
Scotland *Escocia* f es·*ko*·thya
sculpture *escultura* f es·kool·*too*·ra
sea *mar* m mar
seasick *mareado/a* m/f ma·re·*a*·do/a
season *estación* f es·ta·*thyon*
seat *asiento* m a·*syen*·to
seatbelt *cinturón* m *de seguridad* theen·too·*ron* de se·goo·ree·*da*
second *segundo/a* m/f se·*goon*·do/a
second *segundo* m se·*goon*·do
second-hand *de segunda mano* de se·*goon*·da *ma*·no
send *enviar* en·vee·*ar*
service charge *carga* f *kar*·ga
service station *gasolinera* f ga·so·lee·*ne*·ra
sex *sexo* m *se*·kso
share (a dorm) *compartir (un dormitorio)* kom·par·*teer* (oon dor·mee·*to*·ryo)
share (with) *compartir* kom·par·*teer*
shave *afeitarse* a·fey·*tar*·se
shaving cream *espuma* f *de afeitar* es·*poo*·ma de a·fey·*tar*
sheet (bed) *sábana* f *sa*·ba·na
shirt *camisa* f ka·*mee*·sa
shoe shop *zapatería* f tha·pa·te·*ree*·a
shoes *zapatos* m pl tha·*pa*·tos
shop *tienda* f *tyen*·da
shopping centre *centro* m *comercial* *then*·tro ko·mer·*thyal*
short (height) *bajo/a* m/f *ba*·kho/a
short (length) *corto/a* m/f *kor*·to/a
shorts *pantalones* m pl *cortos* pan·ta·*lo*·nes *kor*·tos
shoulders *hombros* m pl *om*·bros
shout *gritar* gree·*tar*
show *espectáculo* m es·pek·*ta*·koo·lo
show *mostrar* mos·*trar*
shower *ducha* f *doo*·cha

shut *cerrado/a* m/f the·*ra*·do/a
sick *enfermo/a* m/f en·*fer*·mo/a
silk *seda* f *se*·da
silver *plata* f *pla*·ta
single *soltero/a* m/f sol·*te*·ro/a
single room *habitación* f *individual* a·bee·ta·*thyon* een·dee·vee·*dwal*
sister *hermana* f er·*ma*·na
size (clothes) *talla* f *ta*·lya
skiing *esquí* m es·*kee*
skirt *falda* f *fal*·da
sleep *dormir* dor·*meer*
sleeping bag *saco* m *de dormir* *sa*·ko de dor·*meer*
sleeping car *coche* m *cama* *ko*·che *ka*·ma
slide *diapositiva* f dya·po·see·*tee*·va
slowly *despacio* des·*pa*·thyo
small *pequeño/a* m/f pe·*ke*·nyo/a
smell *olor* m o·*lor*
smile *sonreír* son·re·*eer*
smoke *fumar* foo·*mar*
snack *tentempié* m ten·tem·*pye*
snow *nieve* f *nye*·ve
soap *jabón* m kha·*bon*
socks *calcetines* m pl kal·the·*tee*·nes
some *alguno/a* m/f al·*goon*/al·*goo*·na
son *hijo* m *ee*·kho
soon *pronto* *pron*·to
south *sur* m soor
souvenir *recuerdo* m re·*kwer*·do
souvenir shop *tienda* f *de recuerdos* *tyen*·da de re·*kwer*·dos
Spain *España* f es·*pa*·nya
speak *hablar* a·*blar*
spoon *cuchara* f koo·*cha*·ra
sports store *tienda* f *deportivva* *tyen*·da de·por·*tee*·va
sprain *torcedura* f tor·the·*doo*·ra
spring (season) *primavera* f pree·ma·*ve*·ra
stairway *escalera* f es·ka·*le*·ra
stamp *sello* m *se*·lyo
standby ticket *billete* m *de lista de espera* bee·*lye*·te de *lees*·ta de es·*pe*·ra
station *estación* f es·ta·*thyon*
stockings *medias* f pl *me*·dyas
stomach *estómago* m es·*to*·ma·go
stomachache *dolor* m *de estómago* do·*lor* de es·*to*·ma·go
stop *parar* pa·*rar*
street *calle* f *ka*·lye
string *cuerda* f *kwer*·da
student *estudiante* m&f es·too·*dyan*·te
subtitles *subtítulos* m pl soob·*tee*·too·los
subway *parada* f *de metro* pa·*ra*·da de *me*·tro
suitcase *maleta* f ma·*le*·ta
summer *verano* m ve·*ra*·no
sun *sol* m sol
sunblock *crema* f *solar* *kre*·ma so·*lar*
sunburn *quemadura* f *de sol* ke·ma·*doo*·ra de sol
sunglasses *gafas* f pl *de sol* *ga*·fas de sol
sunrise *amanecer* m a·ma·ne·*ther*
sunset *puesta* f *del sol* *pwes*·ta del sol
supermarket *supermercado* m soo·per·mer·*ka*·do
surface mail *por vía terrestre* por *vee*·a te·*res*·tre
surname *apellido* m a·pe·*lyee*·do
sweater *jersey* m kher·*sey*
sweet *dulce* *dool*·the
swim *nadar* na·*dar*
swimming pool *piscina* f pees·*thee*·na
swimsuit *bañador* m ba·nya·*dor*

T

tailor *sastre* m *sas*·tre
tampons *tampones* m pl tam·*po*·nes
tanning lotion *bronceador* m bron·the·a·*dor*
tap *grifo* m *gree*·fo
tasty *sabroso/a* m/f sa·*bro*·so/a
taxi *taxi* m *tak*·see
taxi stand *parada* f *de taxis* pa·*ra*·da de *tak*·sees

LOOK UP

teacher *profesor/profesora* m/f pro·fe·*sor*/pro·fe·*so*·ra
teaspoon *cucharita* f koo·cha·*ree*·ta
telegram *telegrama* m te·le·*gra*·ma
telephone *teléfono* m te·*le*·fo·no
telephone centre *central* f *telefónica* then·*tral* te·le·*fo*·nee·ka
television *televisión* f te·le·vee·*syon*
temperature (fever) *fiebre* f *fye*·bre
temperature (weather) *temperatura* f tem·pe·ra·*too*·ra
tennis *tenis* m *te*·nees
tennis court *pista* f *de tenis* *pees*·ta de *te*·nees
theatre *teatro* m te·*a*·tro
their *su* soo
thirst *sed* f se
this *éste/a* m/f *es*·te/a
throat *garganta* f gar·*gan*·ta
ticket *billete* m bee·*lye*·te
ticket collector *revisor/revisora* m/f re·vee·*sor*/re·vee·*so*·ra
ticket machine *máquina* f *de billetes* *ma*·kee·na de bee·*lye*·tes
ticket office *taquilla* f ta·*kee*·lya
time (clock) *hora* f *o*·ra
time (general) *tiempo* m *tyem*·po
time difference *diferencia* f *de horas* dee·fe·*ren*·thya de *o*·ras
timetable *horario* m o·*ra*·ryo
tin *hojalata* f o·kha·*la*·ta
tin opener *abrelatas* m a·bre·*la*·tas
tip *propina* f pro·*pee*·na
tired *cansado/a* m/f kan·*sa*·do/a
tissues *pañuelos* m pl *de papel* pa·*nywe*·los de pa·*pel*
toast *tostada* f tos·*ta*·da
toaster *tostadora* f tos·ta·*do*·ra
today *hoy* oy
together *juntos/as* m/f pl *khoon*·tos/as
toilet *servicio* m ser·*vee*·thyo
toilet paper *papel* m *higiénico* pa·*pel* ee·*khye*·nee·ko
tomorrow *mañana* ma·*nya*·na
tomorrow afternoon *mañana por la tarde* ma·*nya*·na por la *tar*·de
tomorrow evening *mañana por la noche* ma·*nya*·na por la *no*·che
tomorrow morning *mañana por la mañana* ma·*nya*·na por la ma·*nya*·na
tone *tono* m *to*·no
tonight *esta noche* *es*·ta *no*·che
too (expensive) *demasiado (caro/a)* m/f de·ma·*sya*·do (*ka*·ro/a)
toothache *dolor* m *de muelas* do·*lor* de *mwe*·las
toothbrush *cepillo* m *de dientes* the·*pee*·lyo de *dyen*·tes
toothpaste *pasta* f *dentífrica* *pas*·ta den·*tee*·free·ka
toothpick *palillo* m pa·*lee*·lyo
torch *linterna* f leen·*ter*·na
tour *excursión* f eks·koor·*syon*
tourist *turista* m&f too·*rees*·ta
tourist office *oficina* f *de turismo* o·fee·*thee*·na de too·*rees*·mo
towel *toalla* f to·*a*·lya
tower *torre* f *to*·re
traffic *tráfico* m *tra*·fee·ko
traffic lights *semáforos* m pl se·*ma*·fo·ros
train *tren* m tren
train station *estación* f *de tren* es·ta·*thyon* de tren
tram *tranvía* m tran·*vee*·a
transit lounge *sala* f *de tránsito* *sa*·la de *tran*·see·to
translate *traducir* tra·doo·*theer*
travel agency *agencia* f *de viajes* a·*khen*·thya de *vya*·khes
travel sickness *mareo* m ma·*re*·o
travellers cheque *cheques* m pl *de viajero* *che*·kes de vya·*khe*·ro
trousers *pantalones* m pl pan·ta·*lo*·nes
try *probar* pro·*bar*
T-shirt *camiseta* f ka·mee·*se*·ta
tube (tyre) *cámara* f *de aire* *ka*·ma·ra de *ai*·re

LOOK UP

TV *tele* f *te*·le
tweezers *pinzas* f pl *peen*·thas
twin beds *dos camas* f pl dos *ka*·mas
tyre *neumático* m ne·oo·*ma*·tee·ko

U

umbrella *paraguas* m pa·*ra*·gwas
uncomfortable *incómodo/a* m/f een·*ko*·mo·do/a
underpants (men) *calzoncillos* m pl kal·thon·*thee*·lyos
underpants (women) *bragas* f pl *bra*·gas
underwear *ropa interior* f *ro*·pa een·te·*ryor*
university *universidad* f oo·nee·ver·see·*da*
until (June) *hasta (junio)* *as*·ta (*khoo*·nyo)
up *arriba* a·*ree*·ba
urgent *urgente* oor·*khen*·te
USA *Los Estados* m pl *Unidos* los es·*ta*·dos oo·*nee*·dos

V

vacant *vacante* va·*kan*·te
vacation *vacaciones* f pl va·ka·*thyo*·nes
vaccination *vacuna* f va·*koo*·na
validate *validar* va·lee·*dar*
vegetable *verdura* f ver·*doo*·ra
vegetarian *vegetariano/a* m/f ve·khe·ta·*rya*·no/a
video tape *cinta* f *de vídeo* *theen*·ta de *vee*·de·o
view *vista* f *vees*·ta
village *pueblo* m *pwe*·blo
visa *visado* m vee·*sa*·do

W

wait *esperar* es·pe·*rar*
waiter *camarero/a* m/f ka·ma·*re*·ro/a
waiting room *sala* f *de espera* *sa*·la de es·*pe*·ra
walk *caminar* ka·mee·*nar*
wallet *cartera* f kar·*te*·ra
warm *templado/a* m/f tem·*pla*·do/a
wash (something) *lavar* la·*var*
washing machine *lavadora* f la·va·*do*·ra
watch *reloj* m *de pulsera* re·*lokh* de pool·*se*·ra
water *agua* f *a*·gwa
wedding *boda* f *bo*·da
weekend *fin de semana* m feen de se·*ma*·na
west *oeste* m o·*es*·te
wheelchair *silla* f *de ruedas* *see*·lya de *rwe*·das
when *cuando* *kwan*·do
where *donde/dónde* *don*·de
white *blanco/a* m/f *blan*·ko/a
who *quien* kyen
why *por qué* por *ke*
wife *esposa* f es·*po*·sa
window *ventana* f ven·*ta*·na
wine *vino* m *vee*·no
with *con* kon
without *sin* seen
woman *mujer* f moo·*kher*
wood *madera* f ma·*de*·ra
wool *lana* f *la*·na
world *mundo* m *moon*·do
World Cup *La Copa Mundial* f la *ko*·pa moon·*dyal*
write *escribir* es·kree·*beer*

Y

yellow *amarillo/a* m/f a·ma·*ree*·lyo/a
yes *sí* see
yesterday *ayer* a·*yer*
you pol sg *Usted* oos·*te*
you inf sg *tú* too
you pol pl *ustedes* oos·*te*·des
you inf pl *vosotros* vo·*so*·tros
youth hostel *albergue* m *juvenil* al·*ber*·ge khoo·ve·*neel*

Z

zodiac *zodíaco* m tho·*dee*·a·ko
zoo *zoológico* m zo·o·*lo*·khee·ko

LOOK UP

A Spanish–English dictionary

Nouns in this dictionary have their gender indicated by m (masculine) or f (feminine). If it's a plural noun, you'll also see pl.
Where no gender is marked the word is either an adjective or a verb, with adjectives first.

A

a bordo a *bor*·do *aboard*
abajo a·*ba*·kho *down*
abierto/a m/f a·*byer*·to/a *open*
abogado/a m/f a·bo·*ga*·do/a *lawyer*
abrebotellas m a·bre·bo·*te*·lyas *bottle opener*
abrelatas m a·bre·*la*·tas *can opener*
abuela f a·*bwe*·la *grandmother*
abuelo m a·*bwe*·lo *grandfather*
aburrido/a m/f a·boo·*ree*·do/a *boring*
accidente m ak·thee·*den*·te *accident*
aceite m a·*they*·te *oil*
— **de oliva** de o·*lee*·va *olive oil*
acondicionador m a·kon·dee·thyo·na·*dor* *conditioner*
adaptador m a·dap·ta·*dor* *adaptor*
aduana f a·*dwa*·na *customs*
aerolínea f ay·ro·*lee*·nya *airline*
aeropuerto m ay·ro·*pwer*·to *airport*
afeitadora f a·fey·ta·*do*·ra *razor*
agencia f **de viajes** a·*khen*·thya de *vya*·khes *travel agency*
agua f *a*·gwa *water*
— **mineral** mee·ne·*ral* *mineral water*
ahora a·*o*·ra *now*
alba f *al*·ba *dawn*
albergue m **juvenil** al·*ber*·ge khoo·ve·*neel* *youth hostel*
Alemania f a·le·*ma*·nya *Germany*
alegría f a·le·*gree*·a *happiness*
alergia f a·*ler*·khya *allergy*
— **al polen** al *po*·len *hay fever*
algodón m al·go·*don* *cotton*
alguno/a m/f al·*goon*/ al·*goo*·na *some*
almuerzo m al·*mwer*·tho *lunch*
alojamiento m a·lo·kha·*myen*·to *accommodation*
alquilar al·kee·*lar* *hire*
alto/a m/f *al*·to/a *high*
amable a·*ma*·ble *kind*
amanecer m a·ma·ne·*ther* *sunrise*
ampolla f am·*po*·lya *blister*
analgésicos m pl a·nal·*khe*·see·kos *painkillers*
Año Nuevo m *a*·nyo *nwe*·vo *New Year*
anteayer an·te·a·*yer* *day before yesterday*
antibióticos m pl an·tee·*byo*·tee·kos *antibiotics*
antigüedad f an·tee·gwe·*da* *antique*
antiséptico m an·tee·*sep*·tee·ko *antiseptic*
apellido m a·pe·*lyee*·do *family name*
aquí a·*kee* *here*
arte m *ar*·te *art*
artesanía f ar·te·sa·*nee*·a *crafts*
ascensor m as·then·*sor* *elevator • lift*
asiento m a·*syen*·to *seat*
aspirina f as·pee·*ree*·na *aspirin*
autobús m ow·to·*boos* *bus (local)*
autocar m ow·to·*kar* *bus (intercity)*
autovia f ow·to·*vee*·a *motorway*
avión m a·*vyon* *plane*
ayer a·*yer* *yesterday*

B

bailar m bai·*lar* *dancing*
bajo/a m/f *ba*·kho/a *short (height)*
bañador m ba·nya·*dor* *swimsuit*
bañera f ba·*nye*·ra *bath*
baño m *ba*·nyo *bathroom*
barato/a m/f ba·*ra*·to/a *cheap*
bebida f be·*bee*·da *drink*

LOOK UP

biblioteca f bee·blyo·*te*·ka *library*
billete m bee·*lye*·te *ticket*
— **de ida y vuelta** de *ee*·da ee *vwel*·ta *return ticket*
— **sencillo** sen·*thee*·lyo *one-way ticket*
blanco y negro *blan*·ko ee *ne*·gro *B&W (film)*
boca f *bo*·ka *mouth*
boda f *bo*·da *wedding*
bodega f bo·*de*·ga *liquor store*
bolígrafo m bo·*lee*·gra·fo *pen*
bolso m *bol*·so *bag* • *handbag*
bosque m *bos*·ke *forest*
botella f bo·*te*·lya *bottle*
brazo m *bra*·tho *arm*
bueno/a m/f *bwe*·no/a *good*

C

cabeza f ka·*be*·tha *head*
cada *ka*·da *each*
café m ka·*fe* *café* • *coffee*
caja f *ka*·kha *box*
— **fuerte** *fwer*·te *safe*
— **registradora** re·khees·tra·*do*·ra *cash register*
cajero m **automático** ka·*khe*·ro ow·to·*ma*·tee·ko *automatic teller machine*
caliente ka·*lyen*·te *hot*
calle f *ka*·lye *street*
calor m ka·*lor* *heat*
cama f *ka*·ma *bed*
— **de matrimonio** de ma·tree·*mo*·nyo *double bed*
cámara f **(fotográfica)** *ka*·ma·ra (fo·to·*gra*·fee·ka) *camera*
cámara f **de aire** *ka*·ma·ra de *ai*·re *tube (tyre)*
camarero/a m/f ka·ma·*re*·ro/a *waiter*
cambiar kam·*byar* *change* • *exchange (money)*
— **(un cheque)** (oon *che*·ke) *cash (a cheque)*
cambio m *kam*·byo *change (money)* • *currency exchange* • *exchange*
caminar ka·mee·*nar* *walk*
camisa f ka·*mee*·sa *shirt*
camiseta f ka·mee·*se*·ta *T-shirt*
cámping m *kam*·peen *campsite*
campo m *kam*·po *countryside*
— **de golf** de golf *golf course*
cancelar kan·the·*lar* *cancel*
candado m kan·*da*·do *padlock*
canguros m kan·*goo*·ros *babysitter*
cansado/a m/f kan·*sa*·do/a *tired*
cara f *ka*·ra *face*
carga f *kar*·ga *service charge*
carne f *kar*·ne *meat*
carnet m **de conducir** kar·*ne* de kon·doo·*theer* *drivers licence*
carnet m **de identidad** kar·*net* de ee·den·tee·*da* *identification card*
carnicería f kar·nee·the·*ree*·a *butcher's shop*
caro/a m/f *ka*·ro/a *expensive*
carta f *kar*·ta *letter*
castillo m kas·*tee*·lyo *castle*
catedral f ka·te·*dral* *cathedral*
cena f *the*·na *dinner*
centro m *then*·tro *centre*
— **comercial** ko·mer·*thyal* *shopping centre*
— **de la ciudad** de la theew·*da* *city centre*
cerca *ther*·ka *near* • *nearby*
cerrado/a m/f the·*ra*·do/a *closed*
— **con llave** kon *lya*·ve *locked*
cerradura f the·ra·*doo*·ra *lock*
cerrar the·*rar* *close* • *lock*
cerveza f ther·*ve*·tha *beer*
chaqueta f cha·*ke*·ta *jacket*
cheque m *che*·ke *check (bank)*
cheques m pl **de viajero** *che*·kes de vya·*khe*·ro *travellers cheque*

chica f *chee*·ka *girl*
chico m *chee*·ko *boy*
cibercafé thee·ber·ka·*fe* *Internet café*
cigarillo m thee·ga·*ree*·lyo *cigarette*
cigarro m thee·*ga*·ro *cigar*
cine m *thee*·ne *cinema*
circo m *theer*·ko *circus*
ciudad f theew·*da* *city*
clase f **preferente** *kla*·se pre·fe·*ren*·te *business class*
clase f **turística** *kla*·se too·*rees*·tee·ka *economy class*
coche m **cama** *ko*·che *ka*·ma *sleeping car*
coche m *ko*·che *car*
cocina f ko·*thee*·na *kitchen*
cocinar ko·thee·*nar* *cook*
cocinero m ko·thee·*ne*·ro *cook*
código m **postal** *ko*·dee·go pos·*tal* *post code*
comer ko·*mer* *eat*
comerciante m&f ko·mer·*thyan*·te *business person*
comida f ko·*mee*·da *food*
comisaría f ko·mee·sa·*ree*·a *police station*
cómodo/a m/f *ko*·mo·do/a *comfortable*
cómpact m *kom*·pakt *CD*
compañero/a m/f kom·pa·*nye*·ro/a *companion*
compartir kom·par·*teer* *share (with)*
comprar kom·*prar* *buy*
con kon *with*
concierto m kon·*thyer*·to *concert*
condición f **cardíaca** kon·dee·*thyon* kar·*dee*·a·ka *heart condition*
conducir kon·doo·*theer* *drive*
consigna f kon·*seeg*·na *left luggage*
consulado m kon·soo·*la*·do *consulate*
corazón m ko·ra·*thon* *heart*
correo m ko·*re*·o *mail*
— **certificado** ther·tee·fee·*ka*·do *registered mail*
— **urgente** oor·*khen*·te *express mail*
correos m ko·*re*·os *post office*
corrida f ko·*ree*·da *bullfight*
cortar kor·*tar* *cut*
corto/a m/f *kor*·to/a *short*
costar kos·*tar* *cost*
crema *kre*·ma *cream*
— **hidratante** ee·dra·*tan*·te *moisturiser*
— **solar** so·*lar* *sunblock*
cuaderno m kwa·*der*·no *notebook*
cuando *kwan*·do *when*
cubiertos m pl koo·*byer*·tos *cutlery*
cuchara f koo·*cha*·ra *spoon*
cucharita f koo·cha·*ree*·ta *teaspoon*
cuchillo m koo·*chee*·lyo *knife*
cuenta f *kwen*·ta *bill*
— **bancaria** ban·*ka*·rya *bank account*
cuero m *kwe*·ro *leather*
cumpleaños m koom·ple·*a*·nyos *birthday*

D

dedo m *de*·do *finger*
defectuoso/a m/f de·fek·too·*o*·so/a *faulty*
demasiado (caro/a) m/f de·ma·*sya*·do (*ka*·ro/a) *too (expensive)*
derecha de·*re*·cha *right (not left)*
desayuno m des·a·*yoo*·no *breakfast*
descanso m des·*kan*·so *intermission*
descuento m des·*kwen*·to *discount*
despacio des·*pa*·thyo *slowly*
despertador m des·per·ta·*dor* *alarm clock*
después de des·*pwes* de *after*
detrás de de·*tras* de *behind*
día m *dee*·a *day*
diapositiva f dya·po·see·*tee*·va *slide*
diariamente dya·rya·*men*·te *daily*

dinero m dee·*ne*·ro *money*
— **en efectivo** en e·fek·*tee*·vo *cash*
dirección f dee·rek·*thyon address*
disco m *dees*·ko *disk*
documental m do·koo·men·*tal documentary*
dólar m *do*·lar *dollar*
dolor m do·*lor pain*
— **de cabeza** de ka·*be*·tha *headache*
— **de estómago** de es·*to*·ma·go *stomachache*
— **de muelas** de *mwe*·las *toothache*
donde *don*·de *where*
dormir dor·*meer sleep*
dos camas f pl dos *ka*·mas *twin beds*
droga f dro·ga *drug*
ducha f *doo*·cha *shower*
dulce *dool*·the *sweet*
duro/a m/f *doo*·ro/a *hard*

E

edificio m e·dee·*fee*·thyo *building*
embajada f em·ba·*kha*·da *embassy*
embarazada f em·ba·ra·*tha*·da *pregnant*
en en *on*
enfermero/a m/f en·fer·*me*·ro/a *nurse*
enfermo/a m/f en·*fer*·mo/a *sick*
entrar en·*trar enter*
enviar en·vee·*ar send*
equipaje m e·kee·*pa*·khe *luggage*
escalera f es·ka·*le*·ra *stairway*
Escocia f es·*ko*·thya *Scotland*
escribir es·kree·*beer write*
escuchar es·koo·*char listen*
escuela f es·*kwe*·la *school*
espalda f es·*pal*·da *back (of body)*
espectáculo m es·pek·*ta*·koo·lo *show*
esperar es·pe·*rar wait*
esposa f es·*po*·sa *wife*
espuma f **de afeitar** es·*poo*·ma de a·fey·*tar shaving cream*
esquí m es·*kee skiing*
esta noche *es*·ta *no*·che *tonight*
éste/a m/f *es*·te/a *this*
estación f es·ta·*thyon season* • *station*
— **de autobuses** f de ow·to·*boo*·ses *bus station (local)*
— **de autocares** f de ow·to·*ka*·res *bus station (intercity)*
— **de metro** de *me*·tro *metro station*
— **de tren** de tren *railway station*
estacionar es·ta·thyo·*nar park (car)*
estómago m es·*to*·ma·go *stomach*
estudiante m&f es·too·*dyan*·te *student*
excursión f eks·koor·*syon tour*
excursionismo m eks·koor·syo·*nees*·mo *hiking*
exposición f eks·po·see·*thyon exhibition*
extranjero/a m/f eks·tran·*khe*·ro/a *foreign*

F

facturación f **de equipajes** fak·too·ra·*thyon* de e·kee·*pa*·khes *check in*
falda f *fal*·da *skirt*
farmacia f far·*ma*·thya *pharmacy*
fecha f *fe*·cha *date (time)*
— **de nacimiento** de na·thee·*myen*·to *date of birth*
fiebre f *fye*·bre *temperature (fever)*
fiesta f *fyes*·ta *party*
foto f *fo*·to *photo*
fotógrafo/a m/f fo·*to*·gra·fo/a *photographer*
frágil *fra*·kheel *fragile*
frenos m pl *fre*·nos *brakes*
frío/a m/f *free*·o/a *cold*
frontera f fron·*te*·ra *border*
fruta f *froo*·ta *fruit*
fumar foo·*mar smoke*

LOOK UP

G

gafas f pl *ga*·fas *glasses*
— **de sol** de sol *sunglasses*
garganta f gar·*gan*·ta *throat*
gasolina f ga·so·*lee*·na *petrol*
gasolinera f ga·so·lee·*ne*·ra *service station*
gay ge *gay*
gerente m&f *khe*·ren·te *manager*
gordo/a m/f *gor*·do/a *fat*
grande *gran*·de *big*
grandes almacenes m pl *gran*·des al·ma·*then*·es *department store*
gratis *gra*·tees *free (of charge)*
grifo m *gree*·fo *tap*
gripe f *gree*·pe *influenza*
gris grees *grey*
guardarropa m gwar·da·*ro*·pa *cloakroom*
guardería f gwar·de·*ree*·a *childminding service*
guía m&f *gee*·a *guide (person)*
guía f *gee*·a *guidebook*

H

habitación f a·bee·ta·*thyon* *bedroom* • *room*
— **doble** *do*·ble *double room*
— **individual** een·dee·vee·*dwal* *single room*
hablar a·*blar* *speak*
helado m e·*la*·do *ice cream*
hermana f er·*ma*·na *sister*
hermano m er·*ma*·no *brother*
hermoso/a m/f er·*mo*·so/a *beautiful*
hielo m *ye*·lo *ice*
hija f *ee*·kha *daughter*
hijo m *ee*·kho *son*
hijos m pl *ee*·khos *children*
hombre m *om*·bre *man*
hombros m pl *om*·bros *shoulders*
hora f *o*·ra *time*
horario m o·*ra*·ryo *timetable*
hoy oy *today*

I

idiomas m pl ee·*dyo*·mas *languages*
iglesia f ee·*gle*·sya *church*
impermeable m eem·per·me·*a*·ble *raincoat*
incluido een·kloo·*ee*·do *included*
informática f een·for·*ma*·tee·ka *IT*
ingeniería f een·khe·nye·*ree*·a *engineering*
Inglaterra f een·gla·*te*·ra *England*
inglés m een·*gles* *English*
ir eer *go*
ir de compras eer de *kom*·pras *go shopping*
ir de excursión eer de eks·koor·*syon* *hike*
isla f *ees*·la *island*

J

jabón m kha·*bon* *soap*
joyería f kho·ye·*ree*·a *jewellery shop*
juntos/as m/f pl *khoon*·tos/as *together*

L

lago m *la*·go *lake*
lana f *la*·na *wool*
lápiz m *la*·peeth *pencil*
largo/a m/f *lar*·go/a *long*
lavadero m la·va·*de*·ro *laundry*
lavandería f la·van·de·*ree*·a *laundrette*
lavar la·*var* *wash (something)*
leche f *le*·che *milk*
lejos *le*·khos *far*
libra f *lee*·bra *pound (money)*
libre *lee*·bre *free (not bound)*
librería f lee·bre·*ree*·a *bookshop*
libro m *lee*·bro *book*
limpieza f leem·*pye*·tha *cleaning*
llave f *lya*·ve *key*
llegadas f pl lye·*ga*·das *arrivals*
llegar lye·*gar* *come (arrive)*
lleno/a m/f *lye*·no/a *booked out* • *full*

Los Estados Unidos m pl los es·*ta*·dos oo·*nee*·dos *USA*
luz f looth *light*

M

madre f *ma*·dre *mother*
maleta f ma·*le*·ta *suitcase*
malo/a m/f *ma*·lo/a *bad*
mano f *ma*·no *hand*
manta f *man*·ta *blanket*
mapa m *ma*·pa *map*
maquillaje m ma·kee·*lya*·khe *make-up*
marido m ma·*ree*·do *husband*
matrícula f ma·*tree*·koo·la *car registration*
medias f pl *me*·dyas *pantyhose • stockings*
medio/a m/f *me*·dyo/a *half*
mejor me·*khor* *better*
mercado m mer·*ka*·do *market*
minusválido/a m/f mee·noos·*va*·lee·do/a *disabled*
mochila f mo·*chee*·la *backpack*
monedas f pl mo·*ne*·das *coins*
montaña f mon·*ta*·nya *mountain*
motocicleta f mo·to·thee·*kle*·ta *motorcycle*
muebles m pl *mwe*·bles *furniture*
mujer f moo·*kher* *woman*
multa f *mool*·ta *fine*
museo m moo·*se*·o *museum*
— **de arte** de *ar*·te *art gallery*

N

nada *na*·da *nothing*
nadar na·*dar* *swim*
nariz f na·*reeth* *nose*
navaja f na·*va*·kha *penknife*
Navidad f na·vee·*da* *Christmas*
negocio m **de artículos básicos** ne·*go*·thyo de ar·*tee*·koo·los *ba*·see·kos *convenience store*
negocios m pl ne·*go*·thyos *business*
neumático m ne·oo·*ma*·tee·ko *tyre*
nevera f ne·*ve*·ra *refrigerator*
nieto/a m/f *nye*·to/a *grandchild*
nieve f *nye*·ve *snow*
niño/a m/f *nee*·nyo/a *child*
no fumadores no foo·ma·*do*·res *nonsmoking*
noche f *no*·che *evening • night*
Nochevieja f no·che·*vye*·kha *New Year's Eve*
nombre m *nom*·bre *name*
— **de pila** de *pee*·la *first/given name*
norte m *nor*·te *north*
noticias f pl no·*tee*·thyas *news*
novia f *no*·vya *girlfriend*
novio m *no*·vyo *boyfriend*
nuestro/a m/f *nwes*·tro/a *our*
Nueva Zelanda f *nwe*·va the·*lan*·da *New Zealand*
nuevo/a m/f *nwe*·vo/a *new*
número m *noo*·me·ro *number*

O

objetivo m ob·khe·*tee*·vo *lens*
obra f *o*·bra *play*
ocupado/a m/f o·koo·*pa*·do/a *busy*
oeste m o·*es*·te *west*
oficina f o·fee·*thee*·na *office*
— **de objetos perdidos** de ob·*khe*·tos per·*dee*·dos *lost property office*
— **de turismo** de too·*rees*·mo *tourist office*
ojo m *o*·kho *eye*
olor m o·*lor* *smell*
ordenador m or·de·na·*dor* *computer*
— **portátil** por·*ta*·teel *laptop*
oreja f o·*re*·kha *ear*
oscuro/a m/f os·*koo*·ro/a *dark*
otra vez *o*·tra veth *again*
otro/a m/f *o*·tro/a *other*

LOOK UP

P

padre m *pa*·dre *father*
padres m pl *pa*·dres *parents*
pagar pa·*gar* *pay*
pago m *pa*·go *payment*
palacio m pa·*la*·thyo *palace*
pan m pan *bread*
panadería f pa·na·de·*ree*·a *bakery*
pañal m pa·*nyal* *diaper • nappy*
pantalones m pl pan·ta·*lo*·nes *trousers*
— **cortos** *kor*·tos *shorts*
pañuelos m pl **de papel** pa·*nywe*·los de pa·*pel* *tissues*
papel m pa·*pel* *paper*
— **higiénico** ee·*khye*·nee·ko *toilet paper*
papeles m pl **del coche** pa·*pe*·les del *ko*·che *car owner's title*
paquete m pa·*ke*·te *package • packet*
parada f pa·*ra*·da *stop*
— **de autobús** ow·to·*boos* *bus stop*
— **de taxis** de *tak*·sees *taxi stand*
paraguas m pa·*ra*·gwas *umbrella*
parar pa·*rar* *stop*
parque m *par*·ke *park*
pasado m pa·*sa*·do *past*
pasajero/a m/f pa·sa·*khe*·ro *passenger*
pasaporte m pa·sa·*por*·te *passport*
Pascua f *pas*·kwa *Easter*
pastelería f pas·te·le·*ree*·a *cake shop*
pastilla f pas·*tee*·lya *pill*
pato m *pa*·to *duck*
pecho m *pe*·cho *chest*
película f pe·*lee*·koo·la *movie*
peligroso/a m/f pe·lee·*gro*·so/a *dangerous*
peluquero/a m/f pe·loo·*ke*·ro/a *hairdresser*
pensión f pen·*syon* *boarding house*
pensionista m&f pen·syo·*nees*·ta *pensioner*
pequeño/a m/f pe·*ke*·nyo/a *small*
perdido/a m/f per·*dee*·do/a *lost*
periódico m pe·*ryo*·dee·ko *newspaper*
periodista m&f pe·ryo·*dees*·ta *journalist*
pesca f *pes*·ka *fishing*
pescadería f pes·ka·de·*ree*·a *fish shop*
pescado m pes·*ka*·do *fish (food)*
pez m peth *fish (live)*
pie m pye *foot*
pierna f *pyer*·na *leg*
pila f *pee*·la *battery*
pintalabios m *peen*·ta *la*·byos *lipstick*
pintor/pintora m/f peen·*tor*/peen·*to*·ra *painter*
pintura f peen·*too*·ra *painting*
piscina f pees·*thee*·na *swimming pool*
plancha f *plan*·cha *iron*
plata f *pla*·ta *silver*
playa f *pla*·ya *beach*
plaza f **de toros** *pla*·tha de *to*·ros *bullring*
policía f po·lee·*thee*·a *police*
pollo m *po*·lyo *chicken*
postal f pos·*tal* *postcard*
precio m *pre*·thyo *price*
— **de entrada** de en·*tra*·da *admission price*
— **del cubierto** del koo·*byer*·to *cover charge*
primavera f pree·ma·*ve*·ra *spring (season)*
primero/a m/f pree·*me*·ro/a *first*
privado/a m/f pree·*va*·do/a *private*
probar pro·*bar* *try*
productos alimentarios m pl pro·*dook*·tos a·lee·men·*ta*·ryos *foodstuffs*
productos congelados m pl pro·*dook*·tos kon·khe·*la*·dos *frozen foods*
profesor/profesora m/f pro·fe·*sor*/pro·fe·*so*·ra *teacher*
prometida f pro·me·*tee*·da *fiancée*
prometido m pro·me·*tee*·do *fiancé*
pronto *pron*·to *soon*
propina f pro·*pee*·na *tip*
pub m poob *bar (with music)*

LOOK UP

pueblo m *pwe*·blo *village*
puente m *pwen*·te *bridge*
puesta f **del sol** *pwes*·ta del sol *sunset*

Q

quemadura f ke·ma·*doo*·ra *burn*
— **de sol** de sol *sunburn*
queso m *ke*·so *cheese*
quien kyen *who*
quincena f keen·*the*·na *fortnight*
quiosco m *kyos*·ko *newsagency*

R

rápido/a m/f *ra*·pee·do/a *fast*
raro/a m/f *ra*·ro/a *rare*
recibo m re·*thee*·bo *receipt*
recorrido m **guiado** re·ko·*ree*·do gee·*a*·do *guided tour*
recuerdo m re·*kwer*·do *souvenir*
reembolsar re·em·bol·*sar* *refund*
regalo m re·*ga*·lo *gift*
reloj m **de pulsera** re·*lokh* de pool·*se*·ra *watch*
reserva f re·*ser*·va *reservation*
reservar re·ser·*var* *book (make a reservation)*
resfriado m res·free·*a*·do *cold (illness)*
rodilla f ro·*dee*·lya *knee*
ropa f *ro*·pa *clothing*
— **de cama** de *ka*·ma *bedding*
— **interior** een·te·*ryor* *underwear*
roto/a m/f *ro*·to/a *broken*
ruidoso/a m/f rwee·*do*·so/a *noisy*
ruinas f pl *rwee*·nas *ruins*

S

sábana f *sa*·ba·na *sheet (bed)*
sabroso/a m/f sa·*bro*·so/a *tasty*
saco m **de dormir** *sa*·ko de dor·*meer* *sleeping bag*
sala f *sa*·la *auditorium, hall* • *living room*
— **de espera** de es·*pe*·ra *waiting room*
— **de tránsito** de *tran*·see·to *transit lounge*
salida f sa·*lee*·da *exit*
salir con sa·*leer* kon *go out with*
salir de sa·*leer* de *depart*
salón m **de belleza** sa·*lon* de be·*lye*·tha *beauty salon*
sangre f *san*·gre *blood*
sastre m *sas*·tre *tailor*
seda f *se*·da *silk*
segundo m se·*goon*·do *second*
segundo/a m/f se·*goon*·do/a *second*
seguro m se·*goo*·ro *insurance*
sello m *se*·lyo *stamp*
semáforos m pl se·*ma*·fo·ros *traffic lights*
sendero m sen·*de*·ro *path*
servicio m ser·*vee*·thyo *toilet*
servicios m pl ser·*vee*·thyos *public toilet*
sexo m *se*·kso *sex*
— **seguro** se·*goo*·ro *safe sex*
silla f *see*·lya *chair*
— **de ruedas** de *rwe*·das *wheelchair*
sin seen *without*
sobre m *so*·bre *envelope*
sol m sol *sun*
solo/a m/f *so*·lo/a *alone*
soltero/a m/f sol·*te*·ro/a *single*
sombrero m som·*bre*·ro *hat*
subtítulos m pl soob·*tee*·too·los *subtitles*
sucio/a m/f *soo*·thyo/a *dirty*
suegra f *swe*·gra *mother-in-law*
suegro m *swe*·gro *father-in-law*
sujetador m soo·khe·ta·*dor* *bra*
supermercado m soo·per·mer·*ka*·do *supermarket*
sur m soor *south*

T

talla f *ta*·lya *size (clothes)*
taquilla f ta·*kee*·lya *ticket office*
tarde *tar*·de *late*
tarjeta f tar·*khe*·ta *card*
— **de crédito** de *kre*·dee·to *credit card*
— **de embarque** de em·*bar*·ke *boarding pass*
— **de teléfono** de te·*le*·fo·no *phone card*
tasa f **(del aeropuerto)** *ta*·sa (del ay·ro·*pwer*·to) *(airport tax)*
teatro m te·*a*·tro *theatre*
tele f *te*·le *TV*
teléfono m te·*le*·fo·no *telephone*
— **móvil** *mo*·veel *mobile phone*
— **público** *poo*·blee·ko *public telephone*
templado/a m/f tem·*pla*·do/a *warm*
temprano tem·*pra*·no *early*
tenedor m te·ne·*dor* *fork*
tentempié m ten·tem·*pye* *snack*
tía f *tee*·a *aunt*
tienda f *tyen*·da *shop*
— **de comestibles** de ko·mes·*tee*·bles *grocery store*
— **de recuerdos** de re·*kwer*·dos *souvenir shop*
— **de ropa** de *ro*·pa *clothing store*
— **deportiva** de·por·*tee*·va *sports store*
tijeras f pl tee·*khe*·ras *scissors*
tipo m **de cambio** *tee*·po de *kam*·byo *exchange rate*
tirar tee·*rar* *pull*
toalla f to·*a*·lya *towel*
tobillo m to·*bee*·lyo *ankle*
todo *to*·do *all • everything*
torcedura f tor·the·*doo*·ra *sprain*
toro m *to*·ro *bull*
torre f *to*·re *tower*
tos f tos *cough*
tostada f tos·*ta*·da *toast*
tostadora f tos·ta·*do*·ra *toaster*
trabajo m tra·*ba*·kho *job*
traducir tra·doo·*theer* *translate*
tranquilidad f tran·kee·lee·*da* *quiet*
tranvía m tran·*vee*·a *tram*
tren m tren *train*
turista m&f too·*rees*·ta *tourist*

U

universidad f oo·nee·ver·see·*da* *university*
urgente oor·*khen*·te *urgent*

V

vacaciones f pl va·ka·*thyo*·nes *holidays • vacation*
vacío/a m/f va·*thee*·o/a *empty*
vacuna f va·*koo*·na *vaccination*
validar va·lee·*dar* *validate*
vaqueros m pl va·*ke*·ros *jeans*
vaso m *va*·so *glass (drinking)*
venir ve·*neer* *come*
ventana f ven·*ta*·na *window*
ventilador m ven·tee·la·*dor* *fan (electric)*
verano m ve·*ra*·no *summer*
verdura f ver·*doo*·ra *vegetable*
vestido m ves·*tee*·do *dress*
vestuarios m pl ves·*twa*·ryos *changing rooms*
viejo/a m/f *vye*·kho/a *old*
vino m *vee*·no *wine*
volver vol·*ver* *return*

Z

zapatería f tha·pa·te·*ree*·a *shoe shop*
zapatos m pl tha·*pa*·tos *shoes*

Lonely Planet Offices

Australia
90 Maribyrnong St, Footscray,
Victoria 3011
☎ 03 8379 8000
fax 03 8379 8111
email: talk2us@lonelyplanet.com.au

UK
72-82 Rosebery Ave,
London EC1R 4RW
☎ 020 7841 9000
fax 020 7841 9001
email: go@lonelyplanet.co.uk

USA
150 Linden St, Oakland,
CA 94607
☎ 510 893 8555
fax 510 893 8572
email: info@lonelyplanet.com

www.lonelyplanet.com